When Text Meets Text

When Text Meets Text

HELPING HIGH SCHOOL
READERS MAKE CONNECTIONS
IN LITERATURE

Barbara King-Shaver

HEINEMANN

Portsmouth, NH

Heinemann
A division of Reed Elsevier Inc.
361 Hanover Street
Portsmouth, NH 03081–3912
www.heinemann.com

Offices and agents throughout the world

Library of Congress Cataloging-in-Publication Data
King-Shaver, Barbara.
    When text meets text : helping high school readers make connections in literature / Barbara King-Shaver.
        p. cm.
    Includes bibliographical references and index.
    ISBN 0-325-00760-8 (acid-free paper)
    1. Reading (Secondary)—United States. 2. Literature—Study and teaching (Secondary)—United States. 3. High school students—Books and reading—United States. I. Title.
LB1632.K53 2005
807'.1'273—dc22   2005012143

Editor: James Strickland
Production editor: Sonja S. Chapman
Cover design: Jenny Jensen Greenleaf
Compositor: Reuben Kantor, QEP Design
Manufacturing: Jamie Carter

Printed in the United States of America on acid-free paper
09 08 07 06 05   RRD   1 2 3 4 5

This book is dedicated with love to Phil and to Michele, Gavin, Robin, and Will for waiting in Massachusetts while I finished the book. And in memory of Louise Rosenblatt, mentor and neighbor.

Contents

[handwritten annotations: "background", "planning model + order used", "Tells where you can get ideas"]

Acknowledgments

This book is a collaborative effort. It would not have been possible without the South Brunswick High School teachers and students who shared their work with me. It would never have been completed without feedback from the most helpful and perceptive editor I know, Jim Strickland. And, it would not have been finished on time without the patience and help of my husband, Philip A. Shaver.

Several teachers need to be thanked for sharing lesson plans and allowing me into their classrooms: Karen O'Holla, April Gonzalez, Zandrea Eagle, Andre Halaw, Andy Loh, Erin Farrell, Mark Ziminski, Lauren O'Keefe, Wilfredo Rivera, Harry Schultz, Shauna Beardslee, Janelle Duryea, Jill Zell, Stacy Svare, Yoshi Wilson Lassiter, and Dori Bacon.

A special thank you goes to Karen O'Holla and April Gonzalez for serving as readers during the drafting of the manuscript. They are talented teachers and good friends. A final thank you to Mark Zell and Anna Lehre for their computer expertise and patience with a technologically challenged writer.

Intertextuality and High School Readers

R eaders constantly make connections. An image, a character, or a theme in one work of literature reminds us of another text. Some readers read with a pen or pencil in hand, underlining words or phrases and/or making marginal notations while reading. Recently, when reading the marginal notes in some of my books, I found this notation in a paperback edition of *Oedipus Rex:* "Just like *Gilgamesh.*" Along the same vein, in a copy of *Their Eyes Were Watching God* by Zora Neale Hurston I had written, "A female quest story."

"The act of reading, theorists claim, plunges us into a network of textual relations. To interpret a text, to discover its meaning or meanings, is to trace those relationships" (Allen 2000,1). The belief that all texts reference other texts is called *intertextuality*—from the Latin *intertexto*, meaning to weave together. During the act of writing, a writer weaves a new text, while consciously or unconsciously intermingling threads from works previously read or written. During the act of reading, readers weave their own texts, intermingling the words on the page with their experiences, including previously read texts. Meaning emerges as readers follow threads from one text to another.

Students as readers also make connections as they read. They may not always jot them down in the books' margins, as some readers do, but student readers cannot help but access memories, including those of other texts. When an eleventh-grade student writes in her journal that Janie's trials in *Their Eyes Were Watching God* reminds her of those of Odysseus, she is making connections; she is practicing intertextuality.

Although the term intertextuality may not be familiar, it is not a new concept. When people discuss books with other readers, whether formally or informally, they are speaking in terms of intertextuality. When readers discuss a new book with friends or colleagues, they frequently describe it in terms of other books addressing similar themes or written by the same author. For example, a woman asked a colleague whether he would recommend *Daughter of God* by Arthur Lewis Perdue. Her colleague replied, "If you liked *The Da Vinci Code* by Dan Brown, you'll like this book. It deals with the same issues."

Such an informal comparison of two texts is one form of intertextual thinking. In its simplest form, *intertextuality* is the juxtaposition of texts, the linking of a new text to those previously read. A reader's understanding of a particular text varies depending in part on the connections that he or she makes to other literary works. What a reader takes away from a text depends to some degree on what he or she brings to the text. But, as Bloome (2003) reminds us, "Although the definition of intertextuality can seem simplistic, 'the juxtaposition of texts,' the practice is complex" (13).

An Introduction to Intertextuality

But intertextuality is more than this. Emerging from the complex history of literary theory, many literary critics first embraced intertextuality as a reaction to the formalist study of literature, which holds that there is one true interpretation of a text. Formalists, who later came to be associated with the literary theorists known as New Critics (e.g., I. A. Richards and James Crowe Ransom), believe the reader's job is to discover the author's meaning through a close reading of the text. Intertextual studies grow out of the work of the poststructuralists who assert that "a text in and of itself may not have any objective reality" (Bressler 1994, 178). Theorists who support the intertextual study of literature adhere to a poststructural critical approach, one that liberates the reader from the authority of the author. Roland Barthes goes even further when he asserts that the meaning of a work "can never be fully stabilized by the reader, since the literary work's intertextual nature always leads the reader on to new textual relations" (Allen 2000, 3).

The origins of intertextuality can also be traced back to research in linguistics including the work of Julia Kristeva who first used the term *intertextuality* in the 1960s in her study of linguistics, specifically semiotics. Kristeva investigated the relationship between signs and symbols and the part they play in the creation of meaning. Semiotic scholars believe that meaning is constructed in relation to other things, other signs around it. When, for example, a sign says to "bear left," a driver does not expect to see a large furry animal on his left. The presence of the highway and other road signs help construct a correct reading of the "bear left" sign. Semiotic scholars also believe that meaning results from our interactions with the world around us. Applying these beliefs, Kristeva sees texts as "always in a state of production, rather than . . . products to be quickly consumed" (Allen 2000, 34).

As I read mystery novels, I make predictions about what is going to happen to the characters and how the detective is going to solve the case. My predictions are based on the prior knowledge I have from reading many other books written in this genre. If reading is the process of constructing meaning, an important part of constructing meaning is connecting what is presently being read to what has been read before.

The tenets of intertextuality affect both the authors' creation of texts and the readers' comprehension of them. An author's knowledge of texts previously written influences the production of a new work. The father in Jhumpa Lahiri's novel, *The Namesake,* explains the debt Russian novelists owe to the founder of Russian fiction when he tells his son, "Do you know what Dostoyevsky said? We all came out of Gogol's overcoat." In a similar manner, a reader's experiences with previously read texts affects the comprehension of a new one. If, for example, a reader of *The Namesake* is not familiar with Gogol's short story, "The Overcoat," the allusion may not be understood. That reader will have a different reading experience than someone who knows the Gogol story. A reader who is not familiar with the short story may understand that the father means Russian writers are indebted to the work of Gogol, but that reader may not know that Gogol was one of the first to portray the realism of everyday life. Each reader creates correct but slightly different meaning. The understanding of each is affected by previous reading experiences.

When we read a book, a short story, a play, a poem, or an essay, we are reading every other text we have ever read. Likewise, when an author writes a text, he or she is writing every other text he or she has ever read or written. As Chandler (2003) explained: "Texts provide contexts in which other texts can be created and interpreted. Texts are framed by other texts" (5). Familiar texts provide contexts in which a new text is created and interpreted. The word *context* comes from the Latin *contexus,* meaning to join together, to weave. The reader is weaving the ideas from one text into another.

One would think that authors would resent giving readers so much power, but authors also acknowledge and rely on readers to fulfill their role in creating meaning. When commenting on his novel, *The Grapes of Wrath*, John Steinbeck noted: "Throughout I tried to make the reader participate in the actuality, what he takes from it will be scaled entirely on his own depth or hollowness. There are five layers in this book, a reader will find as many as he can and he won't find more than he has in himself" (1992, xiii). Steinbeck's comments support a model of reading presented by poststructuralist literary scholars and reading theorists. So while literary scholars investigate intertextual relations from the point of view of the author and/or the reader, the focus of this book is on readers' comprehension of text.

Intertextuality and Reading

Shuart-Faris and Bloome noted that "while Kristeva's notion of intertextuality is used in literary criticism, it is rarely used in educational research" (2004, X). Although it may not have direct application to reading research, Kristeva's approach to texts does relate to reading theory. The poststructuralists' emphasis on the reader's role in creating meaning parallels the work of reading theorists, such as Louise Rosenblatt who developed a transactional model of reading to explain the importance of the interaction between the reader and the text (1976, 1978). Rosenblatt's work focuses on the instability of a fixed meaning of the text and the role that the reader's response has to the text. She posited that the markings on a page do not contain meaning until readers bring their own past experiences to the markings. Rosenblatt (1976) noted:

> Through the medium of words, the text brings into the reader's consciousness certain concepts, certain sensuous experiences, certain images of things, people, actions, scenes. The special meanings and, more particularly, the

submerged associations that these words have for the individual reader will largely determine what the work commu-
nicates to *him* [*sic*] (30–31).

Meaning is constructed during the reading process as readers
draw on their background knowledge of connections and
meaning, including previous experiences with literature
(Rosenblatt 1978). As a reader connects the words on a page to
experiences, including previous textual experiences, he or she creates a meaning that is uniquely his or hers.

Rosenblatt's transactional theory of reading, published in
1938, and rediscovered in the 1970s, is now widely accepted. It
supports a psycholinguistic view of reading that explains comprehension in terms of a schema theory of learning (Anderson 1977,
Smith 1988). According to schema theory, people activate mental
categories of past knowledge into which new knowledge is
placed. Just as with any type of learning, when people read,
schemata (plural of schema) are activated and connections are
made between what is presently being read and prior knowledge.
Readers' prior knowledge actively affects how a text is comprehended, and the experience gained from reading the new text
helps to revise or create a schema.

As an increasing number of English educators have embraced
this psycholinguistic view of reading since the 1970s, they have
recognized that reading is more than decoding; it is the active construction of meaning resulting from the interaction of the reader
and the printed words on a page. This helps educators understand
the important intertextual role a reader's prior knowledge plays in
comprehension. Readers bring two types of background knowledge to the reading of a text: knowledge of content and knowledge
of structure. The more knowledge readers have about the content
of the material being read, the more complex their comprehension

When Text Meets Text

of the text. For example, if a reader has prior knowledge about the Massachusetts Bay Colony and the Salem Witch Trials, that person will have a different understanding of Miller's *The Crucible* than someone who is unfamiliar with the historical setting. Similarly, the more experience readers have had with the structure or form of a text, the more successful the reading experience will be. If a student has read other plays or seen a production of a play, that student will bring knowledge of how a play's structure works to the reading of a new play such as *The Crucible*. In addition, if a student has read other plays by Arthur Miller, that experience is also brought to the reading of another text to facilitate a greater level of understanding.

Readers, then, create texts in their minds from prior experiences, which build both content and structure knowledge. In the English classroom, teachers help build content knowledge by introducing information, both written and visual, that addresses the subject being studied. In addition, they can orchestrate intertextual studies to help students make connections by introducing paired texts for study in a supportive environment. Paired texts, for example, can be organized based on theme, genre, or author.

Although students make connections independently as they read, an organized intertextual study orchestrated by the teacher focuses students' attention on pursuing connections in a more systematic way. As Short (2004) observed: "Research indicates that although students can and do make intertextual links, the linking is not pervasive in school or encouraged in practice" (376).

Students can make meaningful links to other texts when the classroom environment supports intertextual thought and practices. After visiting students in a classroom in which an intertextual literature study was being conducted, David Bloome (2003) noted: "Meaning was located not in one book or text, but in the bringing together of multiple texts" (13). Bloome further stated:

"Reading is not just what happen[s] between the reader and the text but also between multiple texts and multiple readers" (Bloome 2003, 13). For example, when a teacher assigns a reading of Arthur Miller's *Death of a Salesman* and Aristotle's *Poetics on Tragedy*, an intertextual unit emerges quite naturally. A reading of Aristotle's work with any number of modern tragedies would serve the same purpose. Comprehension of both texts takes on a new depth of meaning as students identify elements of Aristotle's elements of tragedy in *Death of a Salesman*. Reading the two texts as companion pieces helps students understand drama better. This is the English teachers' goal—to help their students comprehend any given text more completely.

Reading theorists and English educators also recognize that the context in which a text is read affects comprehension. David Bloome (2003) noted that the "process of reading comprehension is as much a socially constructed and political one as it is a cognitive and linguistic one" (13). The setting in which a text is read, the discussion with others about the text, and the social and political climate during the time the text is read all affect the reader's understanding of the words on the page, his or her comprehension." As Bloome and Egan-Robertson stated: "Intertextual relationships are constructed by people as part of how they act and react to each other" (1993, 330).

Intertextuality takes this understanding of reading comprehension to another level by focusing on one aspect of the context in which a work is read—how comprehension is created in a context in which texts are juxtaposed. The themes, characters, plots, and language presented in a given story, play, poem, or novel, for example, remind readers of those in other texts. Connections are made that influence how the text is read and how it is comprehended. For instance, students in a tenth-grade English class read three novels during the first semester: *A Red Badge of Courage, The*

Adventures of Huckleberry Finn, and *A Catcher in the Rye*. While reading each novel, students kept journal notes on plot, structure, character, images, theme, and author's style. As the semester progressed, the teacher noticed that the juxtaposing of these texts affected the types of observations the students made in their journals. The students were making comparisons among the works and cross-referencing them. The comments they made indicated that their comprehension of each novel increased in complexity during the semester. Students made comparisons, discovered contradictions, elaborated on previous comments, and raised questions; they analyzed and synthesized information and ideas.

The way students make connections among texts was also observed in a class that Kathleen Strickland researched for *Literacy, Not Labels* (1995). The students in this class were from troubled homes and were required to attend court-mandated therapy sessions that explored the nature of their family and home life. The boys applied this same psychotherapy insight to the novels they read. One day, when discussing *Bridge to Terabithia*, one student noted during the class discussion: "This book reminds me of *Charlie Skeedaddle*." Although his classmates looked skeptical, Gary continued: "When Charlie killed the painter [dialect in the novel for the word *panther*], he did it to get courage to face his fears, and when Jess went back to Terabithia after Leslie died, it was to face his fears" (Strickland 1995, 45).

The anecdotal reports of teachers have been supported by research studies on intertextuality in the classroom. Researchers found that intertextuality plays an important role in the construction of meaning and that students' ability to use intertextual links enriches their understanding of literary texts (Beach, Applebaum, and Dorsey 1990, Many and Anderson 1992).

Shuart-Faris and Bloome (2004) pointed out an important role that intertextuality has played in the field of reading research:

"Intertextuality has guided the field of education to see the complex processes that occur in, around, among, and between texts. Intertextuality has illustrated the many ways in which many meanings can be created by many interpretations and many texts and many voices" (xiv). Hartman (2004) explained this further. In his review of reading research and intertextuality, he concludes that the inclusion of intertextuality into reading research has changed the way we look at the reader, the text, the author, and the context. He noted the following.

> When intertextuality is located in the material circumstances of the text, it reflects the perspective of literary theory and semiotics; when intertextuality is located in the material circumstances of the reader and the author, it reflects the perspective of cognitive psychology; and when intertextuality is located in the material circumstances of the context, it reflects the perspectives of linguistics and sociolinguistics (Hartman 2004, 366).

Because of its complex nature, studies of intertextuality have fallen primarily into three research areas: cognitive processing, sociopsycholinguistic elements, and social processes. Each form of research provides a heuristic for looking at intertextuality in practice. The classroom teacher, however, is addressing all three forms of intertextuality simultaneously. When teachers encourage them to make connections as they read, individually students are cognitively processing the current text by connecting it to others they have read. As they participate in class discussions about the text, students are listening to what others have to say and the connections they make to other texts. When there is a balance of teacher-assigned and student-selected texts, the social nature of text discussions changes.

Researchers are now looking at classroom models that include intextextual practices. In her study of eleven- and twelve-year-old students, Joyce E. Many (1996) found that when reading literature "students used intertextual associations to create, relate to, to verify, and [to] understand imaginary worlds" (49). When reading literature, intertextual links helped students make sense out of and add meaning to the text they were reading.

Susan Davis Lenski (1998) studied the relationship between past and present reading experiences. She observed that intertextuality is "a process used by all readers to one degree or another. Expert readers, however, tend to be aware of this process and use it more or less consciously to construct rich meanings from single texts" (74). For example, a competent senior high school reader who was reading Shakespeare's *Hamlet* was better able to understand Hamlet's dilemma as a form of a quest because that student had previously read other works of literature with this same motif.

Because intertextuality is based on making connections between new and old texts, between new and old information, Kathy Short referred to intertextuality as a metaphor for learning (Short 2004, 376). When we learn something new, we make connections between old and new concepts, between the known and the unknown. In doing so, we build new understandings. In their research, Short and her colleagues focused on learning environments and their impact on intertextual thinking and learning. In the English classroom, their research has been on literature circles in the elementary grades. They found that the social relationships and participant structures within a classroom are essential components of intertextuality. Short stated that "researchers, teachers, and students need to work together to create collaborative learning environments that encourage intertextuality" (2004, 379).

Short's observations about the social nature of intertextual constructions built on the work of Bloome and Egan-Robertson who found that the connections made by individuals are affected by interaction with others in a social community. Bloome and Egan-Robertson (2004) posited that "intertextuality is not given in a text or in a reader, but rather is socially constructed" (1); in other words, intertextuality is being constructed out of the interaction of people within a given social construct.

Classroom teachers need to be aware of how the ideas of others can influence a person's reactions to and interpretation of text. This is especially true if the other is the teacher in the classroom. The teachers mentioned in the chapters that follow are aware of how the texts a teacher selects, the statements a teacher makes, and the questions he or she asks can influence students' responses to literature.

Douglas Hartman's 1995 investigation of proficient readers' use of intertextuality when reading multiple passages found that good readers "relate ideas from their current reading to previous reading experiences." After studying the responses of eight proficient readers using think-aloud protocols, Hartman concluded that the "overall effect of these connected and accumulated readings is that a reader's understanding transcends his or her comprehension of any single passage" (520). Furthermore, students' "understandings of one passage spill over into their understandings of other passages—both past and future—such that a reading is always open to future interpretations" (1995, 558).

This was observed in a tenth-grade English class where students were reading *A Catcher in the Rye*. During the class discussion, one boy made the observation that Holden reminded him of Gene in *A Separate Peace* because of his isolation from the group. When a classmate said he did not think Gene was isolated, this led to a discussion of what it means to be isolated. After a class discussion of this possible connection between Holden and Gene, the second student changed his understanding of Gene.

When Text Meets Text

An analysis of Hartman's protocols supports the use of inter-textuality to increase readers' comprehension of text. Discussing the text that readers create in their minds as they read, Hartman concluded that "readers use new insights from current inner texts to revise their concepts of past texts, and then loop these revised perceptions back to understanding the current text" (1995, 527). Viewed this way, reading can be seen as a recursive process.

The recursive nature of reading alters the role prior knowledge plays in the reading process. In the most commonly held model of the reading process, prior knowledge is an important component of prereading. It is something to be accessed before students interact with a text. Based on analyses of student reading proto-cols, Hartman posited that accessing and connecting to prior knowledge happens not only before reading but also during reading. It is something that is "utilized, constructed, and recon-structed by readers throughout reading" (1995, 558).

As teachers, we need to take a metacognitive approach to the reading process and help make our students' thoughts visible. We can create opportunities for students to stop and think about their own thinking, to pursue the connections that pass through their minds as they read. Teachers can show students how important the linking of a new text to a familiar one is by giving them the time and the tools to do so. The intertextual lessons presented in this book are not research-based studies that investigate intertextu-ality from one of the three research perspectives described here but rather classroom models of how teachers encourage students to think and respond intertextually, Classroom teachers and reading researchers agree that focusing on intertextual links encourages a closer reading of texts. Reading comprehension improves when text meets text.

Intertextuality in the English Classroom

2

One day before class, Will approached his sophomore English teacher and said, "I can't read anything anymore without thinking about everything else I have read." His teacher responded, "Now you are thinking like a true reader." Encouraging students to make connections as they read, to link one text to another, can be a rewarding experience for the student and the teacher.

English teachers in secondary schools are introducing more intertextual studies into their classes because "the similarities and differences between texts help readers produce readings" (Mellor, Patterson, and O'Neill 2000, 39). Shaheen (2001) pointed out that poets use the power of comparisons all the time when they create metaphors, and he concluded that "it only makes sense that we as teachers learn to master comparison, placing different texts side by side and observing the resulting tension" (133). Making comparisons is a form of higher-level thinking. When students juxtapose texts and look for connections among them, they are using the higher-level thinking skills of analysis and synthesis. They are analyzing texts to find common elements and then they are synthesizing their findings into new constructs. Intertextuality promotes higher-level thinking.

Intertextual studies can seem intimidating to teachers who are not familiar with the term, but English teachers do not have to be literary scholars to include intertextual studies in their classes. They don't even need to use the term *intertextuality* in the classroom. As Gere (2001) explained when discussing her pairing of two texts: "Perhaps I could sneak in the term *intertextuality* along the way, but mainly I'd show students how ideas circulate from one writer to another" (171). What English teachers need to have is a clear purpose for the juxtaposing of texts. They need to consider why they are pairing the specific texts they select and how that pairing might improve the comprehension of both texts.

Classroom teachers can build on the concept of intertextuality in two main ways: (1) they can encourage students to make connections to texts previously read or viewed, and (2) they can create a context for the juxtaposition of multiple texts. *Texts*, it should be noted, can refer to nonprint as well as printed works.

Questioning Fosters Intertextual Connections

The classroom teacher is a critical component in students' construction of meaning. One way in which teachers can lead students to make intertextual connections among texts is through the questions they ask, as Lenski (2002) found in her research. The importance of teacher questioning, which Lenski noted, was also observed in a junior English class at South Brunswick High School in New Jersey. The students had just completed reading Ibsen's *A Doll's House* and a collection of essays on gender issues when Mark Ziminski, their teacher, began the class by asking, "What do you think was the purpose of reading these essays in conjunction with *A Doll's House*?" Ramil answered, "The essays offer a different perspective. They don't present exactly the same thing as the play. Some of the essays challenge the messages in the play." Laura added, "The essays are a more realistic way to look at the issues in the play, and they show that these issues have endured over time. They made me think more about the feminist issues." A third student took the question a different way, addressing the reading skills needed rather than the content of the words; she said, "We need to be able to compare and contrast things." Ziminski's students' responses reflected a metacognitive awareness of their own reading processes as well as an understanding of the texts they read.

After allowing time for students to share their responses to this opening question, the teacher posed a second question, "How do these essays connect to *A Doll's House*?" Ramil began the discussion by saying, "Other than the obvious connection that they are all about gender issues, the Tannen [1999] article, 'Lecturing and Listening,' shows the power of words. People put their own meaning into words. Nora's actions fulfilled the prophecy of the words her husband used to describe her, such as 'squirrel' and 'doll.'" Lynda added, "But we also need to look at how Mrs. Linde is portrayed; not all women are the same in the play." These opening remarks led to an in-depth discussion of how the way we describe people labels them; they become the words we choose to use. Reading the essays in conjunction with the play fostered critical thought about the play and the issues it raises.

The importance of teacher questioning in fostering intertextual study was also observed in an American literature class. The students had read Dreiser's *An American Tragedy* during the summer and continued studying the novel during the beginning of the school year. When the students finished reading a second novel, Wright's *Native Son*, in the fall, eleventh-grade English teacher Karen O'Holla asked, "Is *Native Son* an *American Tragedy*?" This question prompted a discussion of essential questions: What is an American tragedy? Who is a native son? Who or what decides what is right or wrong? Who or what defines guilt? How is guilt different from responsibility? Raising these questions created an intertextual connection that helped students investigate issues addressed in both novels.

Journal Prompts Support Intertextual Connections

Teachers can also encourage students to make intertextual connections by providing prompts, such as those listed in Figure 2–1, for reader response journals. The list contains open-ended questions that encourage students to make intertextual links and lead them to consider similarities in themes, characters, plot, and genre. O'Holla also required her students to keep a reader response journal—students were asked to write reflections during and after the reading of a text—as they read *Moby-Dick*. In addition to open-ended reflections, O'Holla encouraged students to record any connections they saw between this book and other texts they had read.

One student, Mark, noted in his reader response journal: "Reading this chapter reminded me of *A Tale of Two Cities* because of how significant social status was during that time and still is." As a junior, this student made a connection to a book he had read his freshman year. The reading of a novel two years previously helped him better understand the one he was currently reading. A follow-up class discussion showed that the connection Mark made to a second text helped him reflect on the role social class plays in defining a person.

After reading Chapters 42 through 48 in *Moby-Dick*, in which Ishmael learns more about the depth of the obsession Captain Ahab has with the white whale, another student in this American literature class responded in his journal:

> Melville elaborates on Ahab's determination and rage for
> Moby when he describes him as sleeping "with clenched

hands and wakes with his own bloody nails in his palms."
Whether because of the blood references or simply the
anger implications, this passage reminded me of Bigger's
rage in *Native Son*. Like Bigger, who encompasses a hate too

Figure 2–1

When Text Meets Text: Prompts for Making Connections

Does this text remind you of any other book, short story, play,
poem, or film you have ever read or seen? If so, how?

How is this text similar to another book, short story, play, poem, or
film we have studied this year?

Consider one of the themes presented in the work you read.
Which other text contains a similar theme? How are the themes
similar? Are they different in any way? If so, how?

Consider a character in the text you read. What similarities does this
character share with a character in another work you have read?

Is there anything about the plot of the text you read that reminds
you of another text? What is it about the plot that reminds you of
the other text?

Can you think of another text that addresses the same major
problem as the one presented in the text you read? How are the
problems the same? How is the solution to the problem the same
and how does it differ in each text?

Have you seen the story of this work presented in another medium
such as film or print art? How is it the same? How is it different?

Have you seen a theme of this work presented in another genre?
For example, if you read a poem, can you think of a play or novel
that contains the same message? How are they the same? How do
they differ?

strong against *white* society, Ahab possesses a fervent hate against the *white* whale, Moby-Dick. Both characters possess a vile rage against a white object of revenge.

Although the student's thoughts are not fully developed in the journal entry, the idea he presented opened a dialogue with his teacher about the dangerous effects of obsession and hate that are presented in the two novels.

In addition to giving students oral and written prompts to help them make links among texts, teachers can orchestrate a formal intertextual study that includes a common sharing of texts. By selecting multiple works for students to read, the teacher establishes a thread for readers to follow. For example, in the eleventh-grade English class mentioned before, O'Holla introduced Walt Whitman's poem, "In Cabin'd Ships at Sea," while students were reading *Moby-Dick*. The teacher read the poem and allowed time for students to respond to it as a separate text. She then asked them to keep this poem in mind as they moved into a class discussion of *Moby-Dick*.

The teacher established a context in which students could think about the poem in terms of the novel and the novel in terms of the poem. By introducing the poem, Karen was helping these students build schema—construct prior knowledge about seafaring men in the 1800s. She was also setting the stage for making intertextual comparisons. The students' ability to do this was shown at the end of class when, after discussing *Moby-Dick*, the teacher referred students back to the Whitman poem. They read it aloud again and were given time to comment on it. The meaning students constructed from reading the poem a second time was much richer, deeper, than it was at the beginning of class, before the discussion of the novel.

One student began the class discussion by focusing on a brief image "ebb and flow" in the poem. He introduced the idea that in the poem and in the novel the image "ebb and flow" refers not only to the sea's undulations but also to the lives of people. The image in the poem reminded him of the rhythm of life in the novel. A classmate, Shea, then related the message presented by this image to the narrator of the poem, referring to the final stanza in which the narrator is applying the sea journey to the publication of a book. The comments made during the class discussion show that not only did the students' comprehension of both texts increase but also their appreciation of how texts are interconnected. Discussions in which students are encouraged to make and share connections enrich the learning for all students in the class.

The impact of the class discussion mentioned here was shown several days later when another student in the class made a journal entry while reading *Moby-Dick* at home. Nisha wrote:

> As I continued reading, I stumbled upon a passage that drew my attention. In Chapter 35, Melville interjects his writing with an explanation, "Roll on, thou deep and dark blue ocean, roll!" Instantly I was reminded of Walt Whitman's "In Cabin'd Ships at Sea." Both Melville's and Whitman's works center around ships embarking on a quest. In *Moby-Dick* the quest is in search of a white whale, while Whitman's poem focuses on the journey of a book, reaching out to its readers . . . Just as Melville commands, "Roll on!" Whitman writes, "Speed on!" Both authors use exclamation marks to emphasize their urgency.

Nisha noted several other similarities in the language and ideas of the two works. She concluded her journal entry with this observation: "The connection between Herman Melville's writing and that of Walt Whitman made me very excited, as I felt well-read and intelligent."

Classroom teachers are always faced with the issue of balancing teacher-directed with student-centered learning. In teacher-directed instruction, teachers decide what works are to be read and how they are to be analyzed. In student-centered instruction, students are given more ownership in the assignments by offering them a choice of texts to be read and/or ways of responding to them. Teachers must constantly make decisions about how teacher-directed or student-centered their lessons are to be. This is also true when planning intertextual lessons. As Probst (2004) warns, the "danger is that the teacher's attempts to relate various works will inhibit honest response to the text" (114).

Both O'Holla and Andre Halaw, a colleague who teaches another section of the same American Literature course, try to give their students the freedom to make connections by asking them to keep journals as they read during the year and to note any intertextual connections. On their own, these students made character similarity and writing style, as well as plot and theme, connections. While reading *Moby-Dick*, Noam observed: "Much like Big Nurse in *One Flew Over the Cuckoo's Nest*, Ahab leads with the threat of force rather than actual force, and that keeps everyone in line." Another student, Rachel, focused on writing style: "At times Melville writes Shakespearean. He uses monologues and lots of metaphors and similes." A third student, Meagan, found a similarity between *Moby-Dick* and *East of Eden*:

> These two books made me consider the idea of hell versus tranquility, or heaven. *Moby-Dick* reminded me of the perpetual struggle between good and evil established in *East of Eden*. Just as Cathy embodies evil and Samuel embodies goodness, so too do all things on the *Pequod* represent different aspects of good and evil. Reading this made me think more about these forces in life.

Seeing the knowledge and pleasure that students derive from making connections encourages teachers to include more intertextual studies in their classes. April Gonzalez, a twelfth-grade English teacher at South Brunswick High School in New Jersey, found that the introduction of intertextual study into her classes was so rewarding that she devoted a semester to action research on this practice. As a teacher-researcher, Gonzalez investigated the impact that "methodically fostering students' intertextual connections has on reading comprehension and critical thinking" (2004, 2). She focused her action research study on a senior Advanced Placement (AP) class that was studying Shakespeare's *Hamlet*. Using classroom observations, student journal entries, written literary analyses, and a student questionnaire to obtain data for analysis, Gonzalez found that "the study of literature was improved by creating opportunities for students to produce intertextual connections that supported both their reading comprehension and critical thinking skills" (13). She noted that her students demonstrated a sophisticated understanding of each text and the ability to evaluate each text critically. A closer look at her findings reveals what students gained from an intertextual study of *Hamlet*.

Gonzalez assigned focused reader response journals that required students to make intertextual connections as they read each act of *Hamlet*. This book's Appendix A includes the directions and sample journal prompts that were given to students. The responses in the journals were then used as a basis for classroom discussion. The number of intertextual connections made in the journals increased as reading the play progressed, as well as the amount of critical thinking evidenced in the students' writings. This was an increase when compared to the type of entries and comments made during the first semester of the course before intertextual study was introduced. During the course's second semester of intertextual study, Eric wrote this in his journal:

"When Polonius warns his daughter about her romance with Hamlet, the reader observes a thematic connection to *Romeo and Juliet*" (Gonzalez 2004, 20). A discussion of this point helped the student understand the universal nature of the conflicts between young lovers and their parents.

A second student, Carolyn, made a comparison to another text in order to understand the characters in *Hamlet*. When responding to the scene in which Queen Gertrude announces the suicide of Ophelia, she wrote: "This brings to mind what occurred in the play *Antigone* by Sophocles where death upon death weighs upon Creon until he emotionally collapses under the pressure of guilt" (20). This comparison led Carolyn to predict what might happen to the characters in *Hamlet*, demonstrating the importance of prediction in comprehension. Neha, Carolyn's classmate, connected a phrase in *Hamlet* to a text she had read independently outside of class. Her journal response revealed a link she made while reading *Hamlet*:

> I never knew this before, but . . . Hamlet's reference to 'bilboes' [shackles] in scene two connects with the character Bilbo Baggins in J.R.R. Tolkein's novel *The Hobbit*. In *The Hobbit*, Bilbo is shackled at first by his own character, and refuses to take a chance or embark on adventures. Later on, the ring shackles him, and he becomes the ring's possession. Thus his name represents his character (Gonzalez 2004, 23).

The word *bilboes* in one text triggered a connection to another. This link helped the student understand that both Hamlet and Bilbo Baggins feel shackled by their own indecisions and by outside forces. Observations like these indicate that when students are shown how to make connections as they read, their comprehension improves because their reading of a text goes beyond a surface reading for plot. The links they make help them develop a clearer understanding of plot, characters, and themes, thus students' reading comprehension improves.

As part of her action research, Gonzalez also surveyed students' views on intertextual study. Sixty-six percent of them agreed that having an opportunity to foster intertextual connections in journals and classroom discussions helped improve their understanding when they read independently. Based on the survey and comments students made in class, Gonzalez concluded that "once students become metacognitively aware of the intertextual connections that facilitate the reading experience, they prefer to continue the process" (2004, 25). Although making connections occurs naturally as a student reads, it is not a consistent, ongoing process unless it becomes part of the classroom behavior. At the end of the school year, after the study was completed, one senior girl interviewed noted that she preferred the intertextual approach to literary study because it made her "think harder about each text" and seemed "more like what I will be expected to do in college."

For a culminating assignment to the *Hamlet* unit, students read Tom Stoppard's play *Rosencrantz and Guildenstern Are Dead.* Stoppard made a conscious intertextual link to Shakespeare's drama when he wrote this play by including some scenes verbatim from *Hamlet.* The play focuses on Hamlet's school friends, Rosencrantz and Guildenstern, who contemplate the nature of life and death while waiting for instructions to kill Hamlet. As David Eldridge (2005), a teacher in Australia, noted: "Hamlet's famous 'to be or not to be' speech is the intertextual echo that resounds throughout Stoppard's play" (6).

In a follow-up activity to the study, after her students read *Rosencrantz and Guildenstern Are Dead,* Gonzalez assigned a thirty-five minute timed writing that asked the students to apply the following quotation by Roland Barthes to their reading: "'[The writer's] only power is to mix writings to counter the ones with the others in such a way as never to rest on any one of them.' How does Stoppard mix and counter Shakespeare's *Hamlet* in the context of the play?" Students responded to this topic individually before there had been any class discussion of *Rosencrantz and Guildenstern Are Dead*. In his written response, Cody noted: "Rosencrantz and Guildenstern present Hamlet's story from another point of view and [it] makes Rosencrantz and Gildenstern more involved, active participants in Hamlet's life. When I read *Hamlet,* I wondered about them."

After reading the students' papers, April concluded that "since the reading and preparation for the timed writing occurred outside of class, there is [a] strong indication that students formed the habit of making connections and prepared for the timed writing accordingly" (Gonzalez 2004, 24). When Stoppard wrote *Rosencrantz and Guildenstern Are Dead*, he mixed writings in order to create a new text. When students read both texts in tandem, they mentally mixed both texts in order to better understand each of them.

The pairing of *Hamlet* with *Rosencrantz and Gildenstern Are Dead* is a natural fit because of the intertextual link Stoppard built into his play. However, teachers can juxtapose *Hamlet* with other works based on their purpose for the pairings. For example, a teacher may want to pair *Hamlet* with Arthur Miller's *Death of a Salesman* to look at the structure of the tragedy or with F. Scott Fitzgerald's *The Great Gatsby* to look at the quest motif. Other examples are presented in Appendix B.

The teachers introduced in this chapter and their colleagues at South Brunswick High School worked on developing intertextual studies for two years. Chapter 3 offers approaches to intertextual studies and presents a planning model that they found helpful.

Planning Intertextual Studies

3

Teachers have many decisions to make when planning an intertextual unit. They need to decide which texts they are going to include, the goals for pairing the selected texts, the assignments, and the assessments that support intertextual reflection. This chapter presents a planning model that teachers have found helpful.

Author-Suggested Selection of Texts

Some authors lead readers to intertextual links by making direct references to other texts. They are consciously aware of other works when they are creating a new text and make the intertextual connections clear for the reader. Intertextual links authors' provide can be inside or outside of the text. For example, when Jean Rhys wrote *Wide Sargasso Sea*, she was consciously writing a prequel to Charlotte Bronte's *Jane Eyre*. When Tracy Chevalier wrote *Girl With a Pearl Earring*, she was creating a fiction based on a well-known work of art. And when Chinua Achebe included William Butler Yeats' poem "The Second Coming" at the beginning of his novel, *Things Fall Apart*, the author was leading the reader to search for connections between the poem and the book. The classroom teacher can follow the author's links when planning lessons.

Andy Loh, a senior English teacher at South Brunswick High School, has his students do a close reading of Yeats' poem before they read *Things Fall Apart*. Loh finds that taking the time to analyze the poem before introducing the book helps students understand the novel and the poem better. In addition, while reading and discussing the novel, students refer back to the poem and rethink its meaning. For example, after reading the poem and the novel one student observed:

> Aside from the obvious that the title is in the poem, I think there are many connections: "the blood-dimmed tide" and "innocence is drowned" applies to the people in Africa when the Europeans came into their country. Also, the poem talks about "The Second Coming" which we learned is religious. The missionaries in the book were supposed to be religious people.

Another girl in the class observed: "We are the beast in the poem. The book shows how all that the poem predicted happened." Because the teacher gave these students the opportunity and time to read and reread the poem with the novel, they were able to work through the two texts. A new meaning emerged from the juxtaposition of the two. A unit plan for *Things Fall Apart* is presented in this book's Appendix C.

Achebe placed the whole text of "The Second Coming" first in his novel so that the title became more than an embedded allusion. The textual source for the title was presented for the reader to incorporate into his or her reading of the novel. More often, however, an author provides intertextual links within the text in the form of *embedded allusions*—brief or oblique references to a source outside of the text. To help them become better readers, teachers need to show students how these allusions are an intertextual connection that adds to the meaning of a given text.

When students are shown the significance of the allusions, they are more likely to look them up. Teachers can model how to pursue allusions and explain to students why it is important to do so. Although intertextuality is more than looking up allusions presented in a text, this is a form of intertextuality that cannot be ignored. Allusions are a form of intertextuality controlled by the author and, as such, reveal his or her thinking. Understanding the connections the author has made to other texts helps in comprehending the initial text being read.

One author who is well known for his use of allusions is T. S. Eliot. His "The Lovesong of J. Alfred Prufrock" poem, for example, contains multiple allusions, beginning with an epigraph from *Dante's Inferno* and ending with a reference to Shakespeare's *Hamlet*. A teacher may decide to extend a study of this poem with an intertextual reading of *The Inferno*, *Hamlet*, or any of the other works alluded to in the poem. In Gonzalez's twelfth-grade English class, students read *Hamlet* before reading "The Love Song of J. Alfred Prufrock." When a boy in her class encountered Eliot's, "No! I am not Prince Hamlet, nor was meant to be . . . the Fool" (lines 111–119), he said: "But Prufrock is like Hamlet. He cannot make up his mind either." This led to a close rereading of this stanza and a class discussion on the author's intent in these lines of the poem. One girl made the argument that most of her classmates agreed with when she noted that "Prufrock is not a king, but he is indecisive. So he claims to be no Hamlet, but underneath he is. He's been talking like Hamlet." Connecting this thought to his prior knowledge of Shakespeare's play, a classmate added: "Yes, but he is more the attendant fool like Polonius." Having the two texts to refer to helped students see a deeper meaning in the poem's lines. It gave them a more complete picture of the speaker and, therefore, their comprehension of it was expanded.

Teacher Selection of Texts

If an author does not provide a direct intertextual link, teachers can select texts based on curricular requirements as well as student and teacher interests. Teachers can organize intertextual studies around a number of topics such as theme, genre, author, or archetypes. In addition, they can plan intertextual units that connect to interdisciplinary and media studies. Because such forms are compatible with what many teachers are already doing in the classroom, they provide a good way to introduce intertextual studies. Chapters 4 through 7 in this book provide examples of the four forms of study. When planning any intertextual unit, it is important to remember the two main purposes for pairing texts: (1) to give students a richer reading experience and (2) to help students better understand each text being studied.

Thematic studies are the most common form of integrated units in English classes. Many textbook publishers include thematic suggestions in their anthologies. Classroom teachers also have developed their own thematic units. In thematic studies, texts of the same or a different genre are juxtaposed based on similarities in the main ideas or issues presented. In intertextual studies, however, teachers approach thematic units from a slightly different point of view; in addition to examining the similarities in themes, they focus on how understanding the theme in one text affects the comprehension of another. Teachers understand that readers create meaning as they compare multiple texts. In a traditional thematic study, students look for how the theme is represented in individual texts. As they read, students keep going back to the theme as the touchstone for comparisons. In an intertextual thematic unit, students begin by noting how the theme is represented in each text, but then go beyond this to see how texts relate to both the theme and to each other.

For example, a thematic unit that addresses the role of women in society might include Kate Chopin's short novel *The Awakening*, Zora Neal Hurston's novel *Their Eyes Were Watching God*, Henrik Ibsen's *A Doll's House*, essays by Deborah Tannen, and poems by Tillie Olsen and Maya Angelou. By emphasizing the connections among these works, students can go back and forth between them, investigating how the role of women changed, as reflected in the literature of the period. Students are encouraged to go beyond the representation of the theme of personal growth in each text to examine how and why each text presents the women the way it does. Students are asked, for example, to compare how the Creole society in New Orleans viewed Edna to how the African American society in Florida viewed Janie. As noted in Chapter 2, when Ziminski asked his juniors to consider the essays about women by Tannen in relation to Ibsen's *A Doll's House*, the students were able to view Nora's role in the family and her relationship with her husband in *A Doll's House* from a modern feminist perspective. This book's Chapter 5 provides a detailed example of an intertextual study that focuses on the Coming of Age theme.

A second form of intertextual studies, genre studies, can be divided into two types: studies in which texts of the same genre are juxtaposed and studies in which texts of different genres are juxtaposed. In both cases, the emphasis is on the genre—the form or structure of the work. Genre studies investigate what differentiates one genre from another and how similar ideas are presented in a different genre. An example of an intertextual study based on the novel genre is the pairing of Thomas Hardy's *The Return of the Native* with Virginia Woolf's *To the Lighthouse* and William

Faulkner's *As I Lay Dying*. When I taught these three books in that order, students were able to see how the form of the novel changed during the twentieth century. They investigated the changing role of the narrator and the structure of the novel. For example, when they began reading *To the Lighthouse*, one of the first things students observed was that "there are no chapters." This observation was soon followed by "Who is telling the story?"

In addition to addressing these issues in class, students struggled with reading stream-of-consciousness passages in the novel. One boy said, "And I thought Hardy was hard!" However, because they had read Woolf's novel, when students started to read Faulkner's *As I Lay Dying*, they were better able to follow the multiple narrators and the stream-of-consciousness passages. As one girl observed when she finished Faulkner's novel: "I'd have given up on this if we hadn't spent so much time figuring out how to read *To the Lighthouse*." These students examined not only the messages in each book but also how the works were constructed. Through the intertextual genre study, they were able to discuss what determines a novel and how that form can change.

An intertextual study that compares different genres could include the reading of Arthur Miller's drama *The Crucible* juxtaposed with a reading of Nathaniel Hawthorne's *The Scarlet Letter*. Although both works address similar issues and have thematic connections, they present their stories in different forms. In their sophomore English classes at South Brunswick High School, Karen O'Holla, April Gonzalez, and Wil Rivera juxtaposed these two works for an intertextual unit that focused on genre. They addressed issues such as how a play differs from a novel and how the two forms affect the readers. Chapter 4 presents two examples of genre study: a single genre unit and a multigenre unit.

A third form of intertextual study is an author study. Author studies are frequently two dimensional; they connect the literary works to the author's life or his or her individual works to each other. In both cases, an author study deepens a student's understanding of text, placing individual texts within a larger context. Juxtaposing Tennessee Williams' plays, *The Glass Menagerie* and *A Streetcar Named Desire,* is an example of an author study based on juxtaposing two of his texts. By studying these plays together, students in Andre Halaw's basic English IV class at South Brunswick High School were able to see how the author's life influenced his work and how Williams included common issues and characters in multiple works. This intertextual classroom study is presented in detail in Chapter 6.

Another way texts can be juxtaposed is by focusing on common literary elements, such as archetypes, in works of literature. Studies of archetypes focus on recurring images, characters, symbols, and themes across time and place. Archetype studies emphasize the universal nature of literature and humankind. For example, the pairing of works containing a quest helps students understand the universality of this archetype. Twelfth graders at South Brunswick High School read several core texts connected by the common thread of the quest archetype: *Gilgamesh, Oedipus Rex, The Awakening, The Great Gatsby,* and *Siddhartha*; the Advanced Placement seniors also read *Beowulf.* Specific examples of an archetype intertextual study are presented in Chapter 7.

Interdisciplinary units offer another way to plan and to deliver intertextual studies, and they often serve more than one purpose in the curriculum. They can be taught by an English teacher, or interdisciplinary units can be collaboratively created and taught by an English teacher working with a colleague from another department. Works of literature set in a particular historical period provide an ideal opportunity to work with colleagues in the social studies department. When teaching a unit on Vietnam, for example, English and social studies teachers can integrate historical facts and primary source material with literary accounts of the war. Literature written during and after the Vietnam War, such as *The Things They Carried* by Tim O'Brien, *A Rumor of War* by Philip Caputo, and *Fallen Angels* by Walter Dean Myers, present the human side of the war. In addition to understanding America's involvement, students learn how literary works are created out of the pain of war. Students who studied the Vietnam War in this intertextual format noted that they were better able to appreciate the sacrifices made for them and others. The war, as one student noted, "now is about people not just boring facts."

Texts also can be studied together based on the medium in which they are created. Media studies are a special form of genre study: They pair texts from different mediums. The main difference between media studies and more traditional genre studies is that media studies focus on nonprint as well as print media. In media studies, comparisons can be made between texts of the same or different mediums. For example, students can view two films and compare how they represent the same story; and/or when studying *Hamlet*, students can watch several film versions of Hamlet's "to be or not to be" speech to analyze the differences in camera angles, lighting, settings, and acting. In media studies, students sometimes compare a written text to a film. After reading Shakespeare's *Romeo and Juliet*, students can compare the written text to a stage or film version of the play. A list of strategies that support intertextual thinking are presented in Appendix D.

Establishing Goals

When planning an intertextual unit, teachers need to decide on specific goals for the juxtaposing of texts. Why are they pairing these texts and not others? How will the pairing of the texts help students improve their comprehension of them? In addition, teachers need to establish how they will know when students have reached the goals. After these decisions have been made, teachers can plan the learning activities. This model of unit planning in which goals and the assessment of the goals are established before learning activities are created is based on the *Understanding by Design* model developed by Grant Wiggins and Jamie McTighe (1998). The planning model in Figure 3–1 incorporates many of the key components of the Wiggins and McTighe model. This model directs teachers to select the form of intertextual study they wish to develop and provides a guide to help them develop essential questions, assessments, and learning activities.

In the planning model, the goals for the unit are further defined in the form of unit questions. Essential questions, as their name implies, focus on key concepts in a unit. As Wiggins and McTighe noted, "Organizing the unit around essential questions . . . provides teachers and students with a sharper focus and better direction for inquiry" (1998, 27). Essential questions reflect the big ideas and, as such, are generic in nature. The same essential questions may apply to many works of literature. Since they can be applied to multiple texts, essential questions support the concept of intertextuality, providing the common thread that connects two or more texts. Unit questions that follow the essential questions in the planning model are where teachers identify more specific goals that relate to the texts in the unit. Essential questions and unit questions help both the teacher and the students by establishing the goals for the unit.

For example, Nathaniel Hawthorne's *The Scarlet Letter* can be paired with Jonathan Edward's "Sinners in the Hands of an Angry God" and Arthur Miller's *The Crucible* to show how Puritan values helped to define the American psyche. Essential questions

Figure 3–1

Planning Intertextual Studies

Course:

Unit:

Texts:

Form of Intertextual Study:

Purpose:

Essential Questions:

Unit Questions:

Assessments:

Learning Activities:

(e.g., "What is man's responsibility to his fellow man?" and "In what ways are Puritan values alive in America today?") lead students to investigate issues raised in all three texts. Understanding how more than one society and more than one text address these questions makes for a richer reading experience. In addition, comparing two or more texts requires analysis and synthesis on the part of students, thus supporting higher-level thinking skills. Opportunities for this way of thinking are possible when text meets text. Figure 3–2 presents a completed model of an intertextual planning guide for Puritan America.

Planning Assignments and Assessments

In addition to creating a context and establishing clear goals for intertextual study, teachers need to give students the tools to do so. They need to develop questioning strategies that support intertextual connections; they need to model thinking that fosters making connections during reading; and they need to create assignments and assessments that require this type of thinking. Some strategies that teachers are already using, such as focused journal entries, can be adapted for use in an intertextual unit.

The chapters that follow present intertextual units of study based on four different forms: theme, genre, author, and archetype. The models are all meant to achieve the same overarching goal—improve student comprehension of texts. The model units in Chapters 4 through 7 were developed by classroom teachers at South Brunswick High School in Monmouth Junction, New Jersey, and are presented here to help other teachers plan and deliver intertextual studies in their classrooms. Appendix B offers further suggestions for the pairing of texts not described within the main chapters of this book.

Figure 3–2

Planning Intertextual Studies: Puritanism in Literature

Course: American Literature

Unit: Puritan America Yesterday and Today

Texts:

The Scarlet Letter by Nathaniel Hawthorne

The Crucible by Arthur Miller

Primary source historical documents from Salem, Massachusetts

Primary source historical documents from McCarthy era

Magazine and newspaper articles about the Salem Witch Trials

Magazine and newspaper articles about Arthur Miller's play

Form of Intertextual Study: Thematic

Purpose:

To help students understand how a shared theme is represented in different works of literature.

To help students understand how societal and personal values shape our actions.

To help students understand the long-lasting effects of Puritanism.

To help students understand how history shapes the literature we make and how literature shapes our understanding of history.

Essential Questions:

What is one's responsibility to his or her fellow humans?

In what ways are Puritan values alive in America today?

How does the period in which a work is written affect its themes?

How does the setting of a work of literature affect its themes and conflicts?

How does reading a nonfiction, informational text add to one's understanding of a work of literature?

continued on next page

Figure 3–2   *continued from previous page*

Unit Questions:

What makes a Puritan?

What are Puritan values?

What is good and what is bad about Puritan values?

Why did Miller write *The Crucible* and set it when he did?

How accurate is Miller's portrayal of the Salem Witch Trials?

What connections can you make between *The Scarlet Letter* and *The Crucible*?

What are the similarities between *The Scarlet Letter* and *The Crucible*?

How do *The Scarlet Letter* and *The Crucible* differ? What makes the texts different?

Assessments:

Performance Assessment One: As the Reverend Mr. Arthur Dimmesdale, you agree to meet Hester at night on the scaffold in the town square. During this meeting, explain your thoughts and defend your actions to Hester.

Performance Assessment Two: As an older and wiser Hester Prynn, you decide to write a letter to Judge Danforth in *The Crucible* to make recommendations for his decisions in the Salem Witch Trials. You know that lives are at stake and that you must write a very persuasive letter.

Debate: Students debate the actions of the main characters in each text. For example: Resolved—John Proctor should have told his children the truth.

Essay: Students write a formal essay comparing the two works on three main points.

Reflective Writings: What have students learned (see specifics in Learning Activities that follow)?

Quizzes: Give and check to determine students' comprehension.

Learning Activities:

Students keep reader response journals as they read, noting any similarities in the works and other links that they can make.

Students complete a chart comparing Abigail Proctor and Hester Prynn.

Students select two other characters and complete a comparison chart for them.

continued on next page

Figure 3–2 *continued from previous page*

Learning Activities *(continued)*:

Students participate in a Socratic Seminar about each work after each text has been read and then one about comparisons between them at the end of the unit.

Students research the Salem Witch Trials and report on a piece of information from their research that helped them understand one or both of the literary works better.

Students use their research to construct a graphic organizer comparing the historical accounts of the Salem Witch Trials to those depicted in each literary text.

Students research the 1950's McCarthy hearings and compare them to the Salem Witch Trials.

Students write a reflection on how learning about the McCarthy hearings broadened or changed their understanding of *The Crucible*.

Making Connections: Genre Study

English teachers use the term *genre* in two ways. First, the term is used to refer to a major type of literary work such as a short story, novel, play, memoir, essay, or poem. Second, "genre" is used to describe forms of literature within a genre type—for example, mystery, science fiction, horror, or romance. The genre studies described in this chapter are based on the first definition of genre: a major type of literary work. High school students are introduced to the major types of literature in order to learn how an understanding of the structures and conventions of the different genres can help them better comprehend texts. Recognizing this, many high school literature anthologies and department curricula are organized around major genre forms.

As students begin to develop an understanding of text structures and conventions, their comprehension of text improves. While studying different text types, students develop schemata that then aid in processing new texts. In his work on intertextuality, Daniel Chandler (2003) noted that the "assignment of a text to a genre provides the interpreter of the text with a key intertextual framework."

He further stated that "each example of genre utilizes conventions that link to the other members of that genre" (5). Robert DeMott (1992) stated in his introduction to John Steinbeck's *The Grapes of Wrath*: "Every strong novel redefines our conception of the genre's dimensions and reorders our awareness of its possibilities" (x). Although there is no fixed structure for a novel, studying the major components used within the genre helps students comprehend texts that fall into this category.

When a reader becomes familiar with the structure and conventions in one text of a particular genre, that reader is then able to carry this knowledge over to the reading of another text of the same genre. This is true for major forms of literature, such as a novel, as well as more specific forms such as a mystery. The form of the text provides the intertextual link. For example, intertextual genre links make it possible for students to read a poem and know that the breaks between groups of lines divide the poem into meaningful chunks called stanzas. Knowledge of text structures and literary conventions is helpful when reading other genres as well. When students are introduced to a playwright's use of stage directions, they read plays differently than they did previously. As one ninth-grade student, Karla, observed: "I used to just skip those words to get to the story. Now I know better. The [stage] directions make it mean more. Like when Shakespeare tells us that Romeo thinks about stabbing himself before the actual end." When Karla reads a play now, she recognizes the importance of stage directions for visualizing and understanding the action.

Prior knowledge of structures and conventions aids comprehension because the reader brings expectations to the text. As a reader reads, these expectations are reinforced or changed. Schemata are checked and revised and comprehension improves. Furthermore, as Robert Probst (2004) noted: "Providing information about the purposes and methods of the various genres will help students know what to expect, reducing their chance of frustration and disappointment" (117).

Genre studies in the English classroom fall into two main categories: single and multiple. Single-genre studies focus on in-depth studies of the structure and conventions that exist in texts of the same genre. Multiple-genre studies compare the structure and conventions used in different genres. In many classes, in addition to reading, students are asked to write in the genres they are studying, for example, students may be asked to write a poem or a short story after studying several models. After studying a novel, they may be asked to write a prequel or sequel to the story, modeling the author's writing style. Pairing writing with the reading of genres gives students the opportunity to expand their writing skills while studying the author's craft.

Single-Genre Study

Eleventh-grade basic English III students at South Brunswick High School begin the year with a genre study about memoir. The enduring understandings and essential questions that connect the texts studied in this unit are presented in Figure 4–1. The students read James McBride's memoir, *The Color of Water* (2002), for their core summer reading assignment. Although the memoir unit was planned collaboratively by two eleventh-grade teachers, April Gonzalez and Lauren O'Keefe, the example presented here focuses on Gonzalez's class. She began the unit by asking the students to define *memoir*. Their responses indicated a range of understanding of this genre. Several students said it was a true story. One boy expanded on this idea by saying it was a biography. A classmate corrected him, "No, an autobiography." Gonzalez did not comment on their answers but asked them to keep these thoughts in

Figure 4–1

Planning Intertextual Studies: Genre Study

Course: Basic English III

Unit: Memoir

Texts:

The Color of Water by James McBride

Selected excerpts from multiple memoirs

Student-selected memoirs

Form of Intertextual Study: Single-genre study—Memoir

Purpose:

To help students understand that a memoir captures a person's life.

To help students understand that writing a memoir is a form of self-reflection.

To help students understand the informal style of writing in a memoir.

To help students understand that memoirs are stories told from a slanted perspective.

To help students be able to identify the genre of a memoir.

To help students understand the challenges of writing a memoir.

Essential Questions:

Why is someone compelled to write a memoir?

Who is the audience for a memoir?

How can a reader identify a memoir?

How credible is a memoir?

How does the form of a memoir support its meaning?

Unit Questions:

What are the characteristics of a memoir?

How does a memoir differ from an autobiography or a biography?

How does the author's point of view affect the telling of the story?

continued on next page

Figure 4–1 *continued from previous page*

Which literary devices does the author employ in the memoir?

In what ways does this text adhere to the characteristics of a memoir?

How credible is this memoir?

Assessments:

Students write their own memoirs.

Students present an oral presentation based on a memoir they read independently.

Learning Activities:

Students work in small groups to analyze excerpts from multiple memoirs.

Students present their analyses to the whole class.

Students write their own memoirs.

Students discuss *The Color of Water*.

Students compare other memoirs to *The Color of Water*.

mind as they read some additional memoirs that day. Then, she explained, they would return to the definition of memoir.

After students shared their definitions of memoir, Gonzalez distributed a packet of excerpts from memoirs, including *Lakota Woman* by Mary Crow Dog, *I May Be Wrong But I Doubt It* by Charles Barkley, *Dropping In with Andy Mac: The Life of a Skateboarder* by Andy MacDonald with Theresa Foy Digeronimo, *A Child Called "It"* by Dave Pelzer, *Autobiography of a Face* by Lucy Grealy, and *Angela's Ashes* by Frank McCourt. Using a cooperative learning strategy called "jigsaw," students read and discussed excerpts from the different memoirs. In the jigsaw strategy, students are divided into small groups consisting of four to six students; these are called their "home" groups. Each student from a home group then moves into a different group, an "expert" group, based on an assigned topic. After discussion in the expert groups, each student returns to his or her home group and shares what transpired in the expert group with everyone in that group. Based on what the students learned during their small-group work, the whole class then constructed a list of the characteristics of a memoir.

Gonzalez was surprised and pleased that the at-risk students who were reluctant readers, many of them identified with learning problems, were able to construct a list of memoir characteristics that was similar to the one she had prepared. Gonzalez was especially impressed that the list the students constructed included comments on writing style. Christian noted, for example, that the "language is not very formal. It is more like talking." His classmate, Justin added, "Yeah, the vocabulary he uses is sometimes slang like 'ain't.'" Gonzalez told the class that the writing they were describing is often explained as having a "conversational tone." Andrea also said that "they include lots of feelings not just descriptions of what happened." The final list constructed by this Basic English III class is shown in Figure 4–2.

Gonzalez believes that if they had read only one memoir, the students would not have been able to construct as complete a list of characteristics as they did. That belief is based on her previous experience with teaching *The Color of Water* as a stand-alone memoir. The intertextual nature of the memoir assignment during this year provided students with more information to add to their schema about memoirs.

For the next class, Gonzalez distributed a brief memoir called "The Pie" by Gary Soto (2002). After reading this new memoir, students met in groups to find examples in this text of the seven qualities of a memoir they identified. That activity led to a class discussion in which students went beyond just finding examples to noting the type of language the author used. One student pointed out a simile and another found a metaphor. Gonzalez found that all students were able to complete this assignment

Figure 4–2

Qualities of a Memoir

1. Based on a true life story
2. Is a first-person story or narrative
3. Includes author's thoughts and feelings
4. Includes a moral lesson or something to learn
5. Includes the writer's opinions
6. Includes imagery and other descriptive language
7. Has a conversational tone

---

successfully. These class lessons led to an out-of-class assignment that asked all students to write a brief memoir. Even though Gonzalez had assigned memoir writing in the past, she had not presented it in this intertextual fashion. Previously, students had read one example and then written a brief memoir. She found that most of their writing was stiff, with no voice and few examples.

The knowledge the students gained from reading multiple memoirs helped them produce richer writings than in the past, including more description and dialogue. Hannah used a combination of simple and complex sentences to convey her ideas and establish a voice. This use of complex sentence structure was a step forward in her writing: "The school system in America was different than Korea, so I had to attend the third grade again. That killed me. Math was a piece of cake for me. Because Korea has such high-standard education in every grade, every subject was easy for me except for one thing: the language!" A classmate, Will, also showed growth in his writing by adding descriptive language— "From the moment I stepped outside, the sun's vibrant rays surrounded my body, taking me into its blanket of warmth." When

Making Connections: Genre Study   • **47**

asked what helped him make his writing descriptive, Will said: "When I reread and highlighted parts of the story [memoir] 'The Pie.'" A third student with learning difficulties wrote a five-page memoir that included language and thinking that was more sophisticated than any he had written before.

The unit on memoirs ended with the students reading a new memoir independently. The following is the performance assessment students completed about the text they read independently.

> You work for the Memory Publishing Company in the advertising department. You have been commissioned to read one of many memoirs available and to create a "new and improved" book jacket to promote the sales of the memoir. As you read the memoir, you place sticky notes on the pages you consider important so that you can come back to them. In order to produce a book jacket that includes a synopsis of the book as well as [a] graphic design, you photocopy two of the most important sections. Using these as a basis for your book jacket, you create an artistic representation of the memoir as well as a synopsis for the back cover. You will present your design at the next monthly staff meeting in two weeks.

Gonzalez found that the results of this final performance assessment for the memoir unit were rewarding. Out of thirty-eight students in her two basic English III classes, only five did not complete the assignment. This was a much lower number than usual for at-risk reluctant readers. Gonzalez attributed this to two factors: (1) during the unit, the students were able to choose a memoir to read on their own; (2) the introduction of the genre using a common core text and several short memoir excerpts gave the students prior knowledge of the genre that they were able to apply to reading a new memoir.

She also found that the work students submitted showed a real understanding of the genre as indicated in the blurbs they wrote for the back of the book jackets they designed. Jonathan noted that "Dean Joy gives the soldiers' point of view and feelings toward WWII." A classmate, Tracey, wrote: "In this book not only do you learn why Larry Bird's life was so bad, but also why he is so respected today."

During the unit, students were also asked to refer back to the *The Color of Water*—the memoir they had read independently during the summer—to see how these other memoirs connected to that core text. One student compared *The Color of Water* to *The Autobiography of Benjamin Franklin.* Anthony found that "both talk about the time when they were kids and problems like avoiding drugs (McBride) or running away to get a better job (Franklin)." A classmate whose self-selected memoir was about Sid Vicious of the Sex Pistols observed that the memoir of Vicious was "done the same way as James McBride. In both stories the mother tells part of the story, but in my book (Sid Vicious), the mother tells every other chapter." A girl in the class noted: "My Memoir (*The Kiss*) is different from *The Color of Water* because in *The Kiss* it's only told from one person's perspective. *The Color of Water* is told from James McBride's and Ruth McBride's point of view." Both students went beyond the story lines to view the texts from a literary perspective. Gonzalez commented that these students generally have difficulty discussing more than the plot or characters in a story; the fact that they were able to see differences and make comparisons was a step forward. Their observations were possible because of the intertextual nature of the unit—students had access to memoirs told from different points of view.

As a culminating activity, Gonzalez asked her students to write reflections on reading memoirs and on writing their own memoirs. Alex, a boy who had difficulty completing the writing memoir assignment, reflected: "I tried but found myself going in different directions. I was also uncomfortable talking about my experience. Also, it takes a lot of work being descriptive and getting every emotion down. I don't like reading memoirs. It's the same as watching those horrible soap operas." In his negative reaction to memoirs, Alex actually revealed that he understands the essence of the genre. A classmate, Keshen, felt differently about writing his own memoir: "Memoirs are a good way of presenting a part of your whole life. It's a way of going back and reliving your life. It helps a person to understand and accept the mistakes made in their past life."

Gonzalez reported that it was worth taking the time to study one genre in depth. The intertextual nature of reading multiple memoirs in tandem helped these reluctant readers not only to comprehend memoirs better but also to produce rich, meaningful memoirs of their own. Reading texts in tandem is different from reading multiple texts sequentially because the emphasis is on the connections among the works.

Introducing a Multiple-Genre Study

A second way to conduct a genre study is to read and compare multiple works written in different genres while focusing on the structure and conventions in each genre. The freshman English curriculum at South Brunswick High School is based on genre study. Figure 4–3 presents the year's overarching planning guide. Although there are unique enduring understandings and essential questions for each text studied during the year, this guide provides an intertextual thread that weaves the individual texts together.

In Jill Zell's ninth-grade Honors English class, students were transitioning from the study of one genre to the next. They had just completed a unit on the novel and were beginning a study of drama. Zell wanted her ninth graders to think about what differentiates one genre from another and how understanding the genre

Figure 4–3

Ninth-Grade Literature Genre Study

Enduring Understandings:

Genre study in literature is the analysis of the structure and conventions of different types of written texts.

Each type of genre adheres to established structures and conventions.

Understanding the different genre types, their structures and conventions, helps students comprehend written texts better.

Essential Questions:

What is genre?

What are the main types of literary genre?

How can a reader identify a genre?

Which characteristics are unique to each type of literary genre: short story, novel, poem, drama, memoir, essay?

How does understanding the genre type aid comprehension?

How are genre and meaning related?

Unit Questions:

In addition to the overarching questions for the course just presented, for each unit studied, students should address the following questions specifically for short stories, novels, plays, poetry, and epics:

How can you identify this genre?

What makes this genre unique from other genres?

In what ways is it similar to other genres?

Assessments:

Identify outside examples of genres

Timed comparison/contrast writing

Group presentations

continued on next page

Figure 4–3 *continued from previous page*

Learning Activities:

Students will complete and revise genre chart

Class discussions of genre with examples identifying how structure develops to meaning

Journal entries

Small groups analyze genres

Read a genre independently and report to class

helps them when reading new texts. Although new to the high school environment, ninth-grade students have been reading chapter books and novels in school and independently since the third grade. In the two middle schools in South Brunswick in fact, there is a program that promotes outside reading, and some students reported reading as many as twenty novels in a year. Zell built on the students' prior knowledge during the novel unit.

As her students moved to a new genre, she prepared a genre comparison activity to help them investigate the structures and conventions used in novels and plays. Zell focused her lesson on the following four essential questions:

1. How can a reader identify a genre?

2. How does understanding the genre type facilitate comprehension?

3. How are genre and meaning related?

4. How does understanding one genre help in the comprehension of another?

The class began with Zell asking the students to write brief responses to several questions: What is genre? What makes a novel a novel? What makes a play a play? How are the conventions and structures of each the same? How are they different? Zell introduced the questions at the beginning of the unit to ascertain her students' prior knowledge of genre. She explained that these were questions for thinking about genre and that, at this point, there were no right or wrong answers. She also explained that they would be returning to these essential questions during the year and revisiting their responses to them.

When students finished writing their responses to the essential questions independently, volunteers shared what they wrote. Many of the student responses indicated a good basic understanding of genre. One student's response was very close to the dictionary definition; Maria said: "It is categories into which literature and other subjects are sorted." Other students defined genre as "a format of a piece of work"; "a type of classification"; "different types of literature"; and "types of literature, music, and art."

Next, Zell used a jigsaw cooperative learning strategy and divided the class into four groups. Each group completed a column for one genre on the genre comparison chart: novel, drama, short story, poem. The epic column was completed by all the groups. Figure 4–4 shows one group's completed genre comparison chart. Since the students had not formally studied epic as a form in previous grades, Zell asked them to use their prior knowledge and speculate what it might be. After each group had completed their columns, one member from each group rotated to another group to teach that new group about the genre. When this task had been completed, Zell conducted a class discussion on what they had learned about genre from this activity. One student referred to the stage directions at the beginning of the play, *A Raisin in the Sun,* and explained how stage directions can serve as the exposition a narrator gives in a novel. This was a useful comment because some students acknowledged they sometimes skip

Figure 4–4

GENRE COMPARISON

Novel	Drama	Short Story	Epic	Poem
• Chapters • Narrator • Usually develop (character) • Direct/Indirect characterization • Literary devices—conflict, plot, imagery • Context clues • Tells a story • Fictional	• usually has tragedy • Dived into scenes and acts • Scripted • Stage directions • Expositions • Direct characterization • Mostly in dialogue	• Short in length • Have morals • Same structure as a novel • No chapters • Mostly Fiction • No minor (only major) characters • More powerful effect than a novel. ← since you can read it in one sitting.	• Developed characters • plot/climax/conflict • Narrative structure of a book, format more of a poem. • Themes • Developed setting • Long poem that narrated the deeds of a hero. • Gods and Goddesses • Like a myth • Verses/stanzas • Tells a story • Fiction	• Stanzas • short (usually) • rhythm • different formats (haiku, limerick, acrostic) • Theme • Repetition (sometimes) • Usually have second meanings • Sometimes rhyme

When Text Meets Text

the stage directions to "get to the story." The students had more difficulty explaining how the genre form and meaning are related. Zell explained that this was all right because they were just beginning the study of genres. She told the class that they would return to these questions and answer them again during the year.

The introductory lesson to genre ended with Zell asking students to complete an exit slip indicating "what they learned about genre today and what they were still confused about." Several students mentioned epics on their exit slips. Veena wrote, "I learned an epic is a long poem and a short story can be pretty long. I am still confused about the differences between a novel and a short story." Jared said, "I learned more about epics and how they look like poems, but I need to know more about them. I learned there were more genres than I thought there were!" A classmate, Amy, learned that "genre is a classification of literature and other forms of art." On her exit slip, Katie summed up one of the goals of the lesson: "I learned that genres can differ and you can tell the genre by looking at the structure and the way it is written."

While working with her ninth graders, Zell found that every time she transitions from one genre to another it is worth taking the time to review the genre previously studied in order to understand the new genre form being introduced. The connections students make between the different genres help them to understand new forms. For example, after presenting the preceding lesson, Jill's class studied *A Raisin in the Sun*. Jill noticed that students paid close attention to the stage directions in order to obtain background information and characterization because they now understood the importance of this convention in drama.

In ninth-grade English classes, teachers introduce students to textual analysis. Understanding different genres and their structures is an important part of textual analysis. It helps students begin to understand how structure creates a context in which character, setting, plot, and theme are developed. When transitioning from the study of one genre to the next, Zell helped her students see how what they learned from the study of one genre can help them read the next. She asked her students to reflect not only on the similarities and differences but also on how the understanding of one form can help with the comprehension of another. As one of her students reflected: "We never looked at reading like this before. We went from book to book and didn't understand how they related at all. Now I can see that genre qualities overlap. I thought they were more different than similar."

Zell's colleagues, who also teach the ninth-grade genre study, found that focusing on the genre form helped students read texts more successfully. Janelle Duryea's college preparatory English class studied a collection of short stories followed by *A Raisin in the Sun*. Her students commented on how the intertextual study helped them see similarities and differences between the two genres. Navini wrote that she learned that "reading a play is different than reading a short story because you don't see things from just one point of view in a play. Also an author uses direct characterization in a play. For instance, in *A Raisin in the Sun*, the author describes the characters in the stage directions before they enter the play." Natalia had another way of describing this difference: "When reading a play, you can get more than one perspective on the story. Since there are so many characters, you can almost read the whole play as one character and then go back and read another character's role. Then you can really feel the story instead of just reading it." By focusing on the structure and conventions of a play, these students read more closely and discovered differences in methods of characterization between short stories and plays.

In another ninth-grade class taught by Shauna Beardslee, students made similar discoveries when studying the same two genres. In a journal reflection, Jarrett wrote: "As readers, people have to look more closely into plays to see what is going on and what the characters are saying rather than to be actually told by a narrator. It is a little harder to read plays because there are details of character and plot and the reader has to read between the lines to find things out." Jarrett's classmate, Sendhya, expanded on this idea: "I noticed that there are many instances in a short story when the author exactly tells the reader how a character feels, but in a play everything has to be more interpreted from the actions of a character. Now I have to make more inferences about how a character acts and thinks and feels." During this intertextual genre study, Beardslee's students learned to read genres differently.

All three ninth-grade English teachers discussed here agree that helping students "pull back the camera lens" and look at the structure and conventions used in different genres improved their comprehension. Before this genre study, the student readers were focusing on plot and character without thinking about how the plot and characters were actually revealed to them. Now students look at who is telling the story and how characters are developed. Understanding the ways in which short stories and plays reveal characters and plots has made their students better readers.

Making Connections: Theme

5

In Karen O'Holla's tenth-grade American Literature class, the students were having a lively discussion about a Stephen Crane poem, "There was a man with a wooden tongue," when one boy observed: "Hey that is just like Holden and Phoebe. Nobody understands Holden except Phoebe. It helps Holden." This type of connection is what happens when the teacher sets the stage for intertextual thinking. Based on her experience with teaching intertextual units, O'Holla believes that students can and will make connections if the teacher models this form of thinking and if students are encouraged to do so independently.

Studies of texts connected by theme are common in many English classrooms; however, not all thematic units are intertextual studies. As noted in Chapter 3, intertextual studies go beyond the juxtaposition of two or more texts; they have a clear focus and an identified purpose for pairing the texts. For instance, a teacher may develop a unit on the theme of alienation by having students read *Anthem* by Ayn Rand, *Ethan Frome* by Edith Wharton, and

The Outsiders by S. E. Hinton. As the texts are read, the theme of alienation is reviewed and applied to each novel.

To develop an intertextual unit, however, readers need to go beyond the surface-level thematic connections to investigate specific similarities and differences in the way the theme is presented. They need to, for example, see how the text is related to the time and culture in which it was written. The three texts just mentioned all have a common theme—alienation—but they present it with very different protagonists and plots. These differences need to be explored as well as the similarity in theme.

In thematic studies, texts are not only related to the theme but also to each other. Intertextual study focuses on the whole text, not stopping at the theme. It involves, for example, looking at how different authors use character, setting, diction, and imagery to create theme. Teaching multiple texts containing the same theme gives students the opportunity to investigate how different authors present similar ideas. O'Holla developed a graphic model to represent this difference, as shown in Figure 5–1. The traditional form of thematic studies presented on the left in this model shows multiple texts with a common theme. The emphasis is on how each text relates to the theme. The intertextual model on the right represents texts that are taught in tandem, with each linking to others. This model represents texts studied in relation to each other as well as in relation to the common theme. The understanding of one text affects the comprehension of another. Links among texts help to create meaning and build theme.

In his book *Response & Analyses*, Probst (2004) warns that there are drawbacks in thematic groupings that teachers plan. But he adds "if we keep in mind that the assignment to categories is simply one reader's judgment, not meant as a substitution for one's own reading of the books, then the arbitrariness of the placement will remain obvious and harmless" (154). When teachers

Figure 5–1

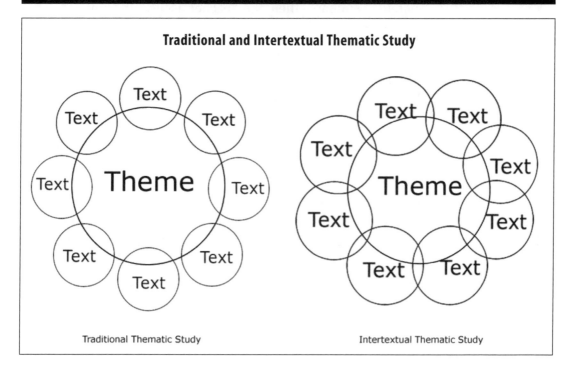

Traditional and Intertextual Thematic Study

Traditional Thematic Study

Intertextual Thematic Study

present intertextual units, they need to be honest with students about their choices of texts and the reasons for them. They also need to be open to student-suggested links among texts. Teachers may, for example, ask students to identify other themes that a text raises and connect that theme to other works of literature.

Probst also recognized that when a teacher plans thematic units "the teacher's attempts to relate the various works will inhibit honest response to the text. Students may try to predict the teacher's thoughts, to follow her reasoning rather than follow their own" (2004, 114). A key word in the statement by Probst is *may*. If the teacher has established a classroom environment in which students are encouraged to go beyond the text to make connections, a classroom in which outside readings are self-selected, a classroom in which true class discussions are held in the form of Socratic Seminars, then the teacher is less in control of the responses. In this type of classroom, the teacher leads from behind by providing the organizational framework in which students can explore their own ideas. A teacher who exemplifies such a classroom is Karen O'Holla.

A Thematic Unit Based on Age-Appropriate Issues

O'Holla created a "Coming of Age" thematic unit. She began the unit with the students' core summer reading text, *My Antonia* by Willa Cather. This was followed by A *Catcher in the Rye* by J. D. Salinger, *Huckleberry Finn* by Mark Twain, and *The Red Badge of Courage* by Stephan Crane. Selected poems by Crane were also introduced into the unit. Karen decided on the coming-of-age unit because it was age appropriate. Tenth-grade students are in the midst of the angst of teenage years; they are testing their independence and questioning adult authority. The planning guide for this unit is presented in Figure 5–2.

O'Holla's students read *My Antonia* independently during the summer before their sophomore year of high school. They were given the open-ended instruction to keep an intertextual journal as they read and to make connections to any texts read previously. In September, O'Holla began the Coming of Age unit with a study of *My Antonia*. Students used notes they had made in their summer reading journals for class discussions. Their journal entries indicated that once they were made aware of the possibilities of making connections, they were able to do so.

One student, Prasanthi, made connections among *My Antonia* and several other texts; she found that the "same theme of overcoming obstacles was in *The Odyssey*." She also noted that a "similar

Figure 5–2

Planning Intertextual Studies: Theme Study

Course: English II Honors

Unit: American Literature

Texts:

The Adventures of Huckleberry Finn by Mark Twain

The Red Badge of Courage by Stephen Crane

The Catcher in the Rye by J. D. Salinger

My Antonia by Willa Cather

Selected poetry of Stephen Crane

Form of Intertextual Study: Theme—Coming of Age

Thematic Statement: All people go through a rite of passage.

Purpose:

To help students understand how a study of multiple works containing the same theme can lead to a better understanding of each one.

To help students understand how an author uses literary devices to build theme.

To help students understand the universal nature of recurring themes.

To help students identify theme in a text and use evidence to support their claims.

Essential Questions:

How are coming-of-age stories similar across cultures and societies?

How is loss of innocence connected to a coming-of-age story?

What does a coming-of-age story reveal about life?

How can a coming-of-age story be both a physical and a mental journey?

Why do coming-of-age stories endure?

continued on next page

Figure 5–2 *continued from previous page*

Unit Questions:

Which characteristics do these coming-of-age stories share?

How are they different?

How are the challenges the protagonists face similar?

What do the protagonists have in common?

What determines the effect these challenges have on the protagonists?

How does poetry demonstrate the universality of the coming-of-age theme?

Learning Activities:

Journal entries

Socratic Seminars

Class discussions

Cooperative group analyses of characters, including completion of graphic organizers

Assessments:

Socratic Seminar discussion

Literary analysis essay—character analysis

Personal narrative—connect own life to events and characters in story

Journal entries

Comprehension test

Performance Assessment:

Psychiatric Profile of Holden Caulfield

As a psychiatrist on a team of professionals evaluating Holden Caulfield, you and your team need to write a complete diagnostic evaluation of your patient. Your team's diagnosis needs to be based on the evidence you collect from the patient, his observed behavior, and his family. Your team's diagnosis is also to be based on your combined expertise in the area of psychiatric disorders. Once a diagnosis is reached, you need to write a letter to his parents stating your findings and suggesting a treatment plan.

theme of prejudice was in *A Raisin in the Sun*." A classmate, Laura, was able to make connections to issues, imagery, and characters in other texts. Laura connected *My Antonia* to *Stargirl* by Jerry Spinelli, noting that the characters in both books are "looked down upon because of their strange customs." She also connected *My Antonia* to *Romeo and Juliet* by comparing the imagery the authors employ. She said that "both Willa Cather and William Shakespeare utilize imagery involving the sun and the moon in order to aid plot development." Finally, Laura noted similarities between the characters in *My Antonia* and *Running Out of Time* by Margaret Petersen Haddix: "Both are intelligent young women who want to learn more about life. . . . Not only are their characteristics the same, but they both make similar choices for the same reasons. Antonia and Jesse both become better people because they choose to think not of themselves, but of the people they love." As she read *My Antonia*, Laura was able to revisit texts she had read previously and make comparisons on many levels.

O'Holla offers a caveat for teachers who are beginning intertextual study in their classrooms: Teachers need to first model what is meant by intertextual links; otherwise, students looking for connections in a text they are reading frequently stop at the personal level. Believing he was making an intertextual connection, one student wrote: "My Antonia is the same as what happened to my family when they came to America." Although the classroom teacher does not want to stifle personal connections students make with texts, it is important for them to understand the nature of intertextual thinking.

In class, O'Holla began a discussion of *My Antonia* by asking the students to finish this sentence: *My Antonia* is about . . . . The students brainstormed ideas and created this list: friendship, the importance of memory, relationships, loss of innocence, growing up.

Because students had read the book and thought about the thematic issues it raises, they had developed a schema for coming-of-age literature that they were ready to apply to new texts.

When studying *The Catcher in the Rye*, O'Holla also introduced selected poetry by Stephen Crane. They read "A learned man came to me once," "The wayfarer," and "There was a man with a tongue of wood." The introduction of Crane's poetry served two purposes: (1) it enhanced the universal nature of the coming-of-age theme, and (2) it introduced an author whose novel the students would be reading later in the unit. During class discussions throughout the unit, O'Holla noted that students independently returned to these poems. For example, at the beginning of the study of *Huckleberry Finn*, O'Holla asked students to consider how they would fill in the blank in this poem: "The _____ Speaks of Rivers" by Huck Finn. The class responded without any prompts; they had not yet read "The Negro Speaks of Rivers" by Langston Hughes when O'Holla assigned this topic. (They were to read the Hughes poem after studying *Huckleberry Finn*.)

Students responded to O'Holla's prompt by filling in the blank with "the boy," "the outcast," "the runaway." One student, Kamal, said "the wayfarer because Huck is the wayfarer like in Crane's poem." O'Holla followed this comment by asking for an explanation of the connection. Emily noted that "when Huck goes ashore he has negative experiences, but when he comes back, he has grown, has learned something. " Kamal added, "As he looses his innocence, he changes. Loss of innocence is not all negative; it sounds negative. It is not negative if you then become a better person." Understanding Crane's poem before reading *Huckleberry Finn* helped these students see more in the actions of the protagonist.

At the beginning of the Coming of Age unit, students were prompted to make connections to other works they had read, but, as the unit progressed, O'Holla found that they no longer needed any prompting. Her students were making intertextual connections independently. At the end of the unit, students reflected on what they had learned and many commented on how the intertextual nature of the unit helped them comprehend the theme. Maryam found that "looking at different authors' use of imagery helped me see how the theme was accomplished. Reading the theme in several books and poems enhanced my comprehension of 'coming of age.' Previously I viewed it as a literal change in age. Now 'coming of age' means self-discovery and finding one's conscience."

Sonia also noticed the authors' use of imagery: "To each of these characters mother nature provided shelter or a sense of sanctuary to make them feel at home." Jordan observed the overall impact of studying a thematic unit intertextually: "Studying literature by themes helps in my understanding by providing different insights into different works. Analyzing the reasons behind the differences among works forces me to look at the works from alternative view-points." Paul summed up his reading experience this way:

> After reading many works, certain ideas started making sense. For example, every main character had a companion except for Henry in *The Red Badge of Courage.* The lack of [a] companion could explain some of Henry's actions. Henry did not have anyone to help him get through extra tough times. This could bring out the theme that friends are needed to help each other go through life's obstacles. This [theme] couldn't have been reached without comparing these novels.

These students and their classmates benefited from studying multiple works in an intertextual fashion. It stretched their thinking and prompted them not only to identify themes but also to look for how themes are created.

A Thematic Unit Based on Available Texts

In *Response & Analysis* (2004), Probst noted that many of the decisions concerning which books will be studied in an English classroom depend on the books that are available at the school. South Brunswick High School eleventh-grade English teachers were looking for a way to plan an intertextual study based on theme. As they reviewed available works, they saw a common theme emerge from the texts themselves: "Insiders and Outsiders." Using this theme as a guide, they developed the following overarching essential questions that would focus the year-long thematic study.

- Why are there insiders and outsiders in any society and/or social group?

- Who or what qualifies an individual as an insider or an outsider?

- What are the advantages and the disadvantages of being an insider or an outsider?

- Under what circumstances might the roles of the insider and/or the outsider be reversed or changed?

- What is the effect of a change from one to the other?

The core texts teachers included were *The Color of Water* by James McBride, *One Flew Over the Cuckoo's Nest* by Ken Kesey, *Their Eyes Were Watching God* by Zora Neale Hurston, *Macbeth* by William Shakespeare, and *The Metamorphosis* by Franz Kafka. Some teachers substituted *The Taming of the Shrew* by Shakespeare for *Macbeth*. These core works were supplemented with shorter texts that addressed the same theme. Each teacher and his or her class chose different stories, poems, essays, and films to study in addition to the core works.

Approaching the works from the point of view of Insiders and Outsiders led to rich discussions of issues that went beyond the classroom to generalizations about life. For example, students who struggled with some of the readings realized at the end that an outsider can challenge and change the status quo, as exemplified by McMurphy in *One Flew Over the Cuckoo's Nest*, Janie in *Their Eyes Were Watching God*, and James in *The Color of Water*. When students compared McMurphy to Macbeth, they also learned that outsiders can have positive or negative motivations for their actions. As one girl noted, "Not all outsiders deserve to be insiders."

After reading three Insider and Outsider theme study texts—*The Color of Water, 1984*, and *Their Eyes Were Watching God*—Zandrea Eagle asked her eleventh graders what the novels had in common and how reading them together helped their understanding of each. Rich found that "all three of these books showed the personal battle of the self-discoveries of the main characters." Mike added: "These books all deal with the suppression of people. The characters also have to struggle to find themselves. I found it easier to stay focused when I read the books on the same theme. It helps to have backup books. It is easier to comprehend when they all relate." Amira noted that reading the novels together helped her "see how different characters go through the same feelings and experiences." Kim also found that by reading *Their Eyes Were Watching God* in conjunction with *The Color of Water* she could "make comparisons and see how the times changed for African Americans." Jasleen summed up the theme in her written reflection:

All three novels have the same theme: individuals in any society are often controlled by someone. James in *The Color of Water* had restrictions put on him and was controlled because he was African American. Winston in *1984* was controlled by the totalitarian government [that] monitored his actions. And in *Their Eyes Were Watching God*, Janie was controlled by her husbands.

In the past, students who had read these three books in isolation during the school year had not made the thematic connections these students did. Their understanding of the theme was enhanced by the intertextual readings. Dominic commented on this when he explained that reading the books together "helped me because it kept the memory of the stories fresh in your head so that you could relate to each of the books and make comparisons."

Eagle's goal for developing an intertextual unit based on these three books was to help students understand the Insiders and Outsiders theme, to see the different ways the oppression of people can occur. The students' oral and written comments indicated that this goal was reached. Eagle noted that in the past when she taught *Their Eyes Were Watching God* in isolation, students had difficulty seeing beyond, as one student once said, "the soap opera love story" to understanding the larger issues in the book such as the oppression of women. Connecting this text thematically to others helped her students understand a major theme in the novel.

Another junior English teacher, Lauren O'Keefe, also taught the Insiders and Outsiders thematic unit. O'Keefe's students were able to identify insiders and outsiders in the major works they read and support their observations with specific quotations from the texts. For example, when studying *The Color of Water*, Vraj noted that Ruth, a Jewish woman married to a black man, felt like an outsider when she was learning to dance, "but some of the girls made such a fuss over having to dance with a Jew that I dropped out of it" (McBride 2002, 108). On the other hand, Ruth felt like an insider when she was with the black community "maybe because I'd lived around black folks most of my life" (171). Vraj and his classmates discussed how Ruth was an outsider and insider in two communities—the Jewish one into which she was born and the black one into which she married. Juli noted that Ruth's son, James, was also an outsider and an insider. James was half-black, and "felt like an outsider in both worlds, especially when his mother placed him into a predominantly Jewish school." Discussing quotations, such as these from *The Color of Water,* helped students understand that a society can label someone an outsider or an insider based on a person's religion or skin color.

During the thematic study, O'Keefe's students addressed the essential questions: Why are there insiders and outsiders in a society? What are the advantages and the disadvantages of being an insider or an outsider? Under what circumstances might the roles of the insider and the outsider be reversed or changed? In response to the questions, Tabitha noted: "It is society's nature to have norms. People who accept these norms are insiders and everyone else is an outsider." Juli agreed but added: "Yet people disagree about what may be 'in'." Concerning the advantages of being in one group or the other, Lauren's students tended to agree that there is a lot of pressure to be in the "in" group, and that you feel "well-liked if you are an insider." However, they also saw difficulties with being an insider. As Juli stated, "Sometimes you don't know who really likes you for being you or being in the 'in' group. The advantage of being an outsider is that you are not in the spotlight all the time." Stephen saw that a disadvantage of being an outsider was that they tended to be stereotyped. Juli also commented on how the roles can change: "The roles of an insider or outsider may reverse when the outsider is better at something than the insider and becomes well-liked for it." Sara agreed that the roles can change and added that the "outsiders' perception of themselves might also change."

The discussions based on the essential questions raised important issues in the lives of these adolescents. Many students had personal examples to support their views of insiders and outsiders. Understanding the thematic issues on a personal level helped the students better comprehend the issues raised in the literature. They were able to make the transition from their personal examples to the situations in the literature. Chris, for example, found that being an outsider taught that "you don't need friends to survive. This is like James in *The Color of Water*. . . . However," Chris added, "you may be lonely."

Later in the year, O'Keefe asked her students to reflect on the connections among the texts they had been reading during the Insiders and Outsiders thematic unit. She was impressed with her students' ability to connect such seemingly unlikely works as *Macbeth* and *The Color of Water*. Without any teacher prompting, Megan noted:

> Both *Macbeth* and *The Color of Water* include quests for something greater, tales of ambition. *Macbeth* craves to be greater than he is. He does anything to become King, even killing his best friend. In *The Color of Water*, James McBride explains his quest for something greater in reference to acceptance and comfort with his own identity. He wants to feel better than he already does.

Without using the terms *insider* or *outsider*, Megan expressed the theme that people feel cut off from the power and look for ways to get it. Jackie noted the same connection: "Both James and Macbeth are fixated with their roles in society. They are both searching for their own identity."

Several students in the class commented on how reading the two works within the same unit helped them comprehend both.

Romell found that "by reading the two closely together, I've been able to get a better understanding of analyzing abstract text. I find a play confusing, but having first read a story with the same theme which is written in the first person, I was better able to read and understand the play." Dan found that reading the two together helped him understand "how the characters have a motive and think and work." O'Keefe's students, like Eagle's, were able to comprehend multiple texts better by comparing them to each other.

As shown in the preceding two models, when planning thematic intertextual studies, teachers can begin with a theme in mind and look for works that support that theme; or, they can begin with a review of the texts they own and look for themes that are represented in those texts. In either case, the thematic thread that is followed from one text to another gives students opportunities to make connections among texts and to think about them in multiple ways. Connecting and revisiting texts improves students' understanding of the themes and the texts in which the themes are represented.

Making Connections:
Author Study

6

At the beginning of class, seniors in Andre Halaw's basic English IV course at South Brunswick High School are busy writing in their journals, responding to a prompt he has written on the board: Who does Blanche resemble from *The Glass Menagerie*? This lesson is part of an author study on the life and works of Tennessee Williams. For six weeks, these basic English students, many of them reluctant readers, are reading multiple works by and about Tennessee Williams.

Author studies that include reading multiple works written by the same author center around two forms of intertextuality—(1) connections between an author's life and his works and (2) connections among texts. The teacher's role is to provide students with the resources needed to make these connections. For example, teachers need to plan ways to incorporate the author's life into the study that go beyond prereading the biographical information included in many anthologies. In author studies, purposeful connections need to be made between an author's life and his or her work.

As Harry Schultz, an English teacher and dramatist who wrote the play, *Blanche's Chair in the Moon*, based on Williams' life, explained: "Tales of an author's life are embellished and transformed to create art. In an author study, understanding an author's life is an important part of interpreting his work. When focusing on the author's background, readers need to consider: Why is this text being created out of this biographical moment in time and location?" (Personal interview September, 2004). He goes on to explain that Williams was able, for example, to address taboo subjects, which he could not present overtly in America during the 1940s and 1950s, in his art.

Recognizing the importance of including both the author's life and multiple texts in an author study, Halaw included both in his intertextual unit on Tennessee Williams (Figure 6–1). Halaw wanted to begin the unit by using a contemporary character whom the students would recognize. When working with reluctant readers, he understood that teachers need to make connections to the students' world whenever possible. When these students are able to tap into their prior knowledge and/or make a personal connection before or during reading, their motivation for reading and comprehension of the text improves. With this in mind, Halaw began his author study of Tennessee Williams with an unlikely choice—a film clip from *Pee Wee Herman's Big Adventure*. He showed a scene in which Pee Wee demonstrates his fondness for the possessions in his life that ends with Pee Wee's adoration of his bicycle. This teacher then asked his students to reflect in their journals about the danger of living like this. One student responded that the problem is "living for something not for yourself." A classmate added that "having things is what it's all about not people." When students finished sharing their responses, Halaw explained that they were going to be reading a play in which a character has a collection of glass animals that are the focus of

When Text Meets Text

Figure 6–1

Planning Intertextual Studies: Author Study

Course: Basic English IV

Unit: Modern American Literature

Texts:

A Streetcar Named Desire by Tennessee Williams

The Glass Menagerie by Tennessee Williams

Blanche's Chair in the Moon by Harry Schultz

Poem: "Life Story" by Tennessee Williams

Video: *Tennessee Williams: Orpheus of the American Stage* (PBS, 12/19/94)

Excerpts from *The Things They Carried* by Tim O'Brien

Form of Intertextual Study: Author study

Purpose:

To help students understand how a study of multiple works by the same author can lead to a better understanding of each one.

To help students understand how an author's life is often reflected in his or her works.

To help students understand the evolution of a text.

To help students understand common themes, motifs, symbols, and characters presented in multiple works written by Tennessee Williams.

Essential Questions:

How does understanding an author's life help a reader understand his or her work?

How can reading multiple works reveal more about an author and his or her works than reading one single text?

Unit Questions:

How much of Williams' life is represented in *A Streetcar Named Desire*?

How much of Williams' life is represented in *A Glass Menagerie*?

continued on next page

Figure 6–1 *continued from previous page*

Unit Questions *(continued)*:

Which themes, symbols, and characters in *A Streetcar Named Desire* are connected in some way to those in *A Glass Menagerie*?

In what ways are Williams' poems related to his plays?

How does reading a play about the life and works of Williams help in the comprehension of two of his plays?

Learning Activities:

Journal entries

Outside readings: Excerpts from *The Things They Carried*

Essay by Stephen King: "Why We Crave Horror Movies"

Written comparison of characters

Class discussions

Analysis of Williams' poem, "Life Story"

View video: *Tennessee Williams: Orpheus of the American Stage*

Assessments:

Journal entries

Unit test

Written comparison of characters

Group analysis of Williams' poem, "Life Story"

Performance Assessment:

You are a scriptwriter proposing a new play based on the life and works of Tennessee Williams. Working in teams of three, you and your colleagues are to prepare a scripted conversation to show the production company. You should plan to include Williams in a scene in which he has a conversation with a character from *The Glass Menagerie* and a character from *A Streetcar Named Desire*. Your script needs to impress the production company with your knowledge of Williams' life and works.

her life. He asked students to keep this discussion in mind as they read the play.

During their study of *The Glass Menagerie*, students were asked to keep a reader response journal and to make two entries for every scene. They were told their entries should include vocabulary that was new and observations about characters. In addition, Andre gave the class daily prompts to respond to in their journals. Many of the prompts encouraged students to make connections as they read. Based on his experience with the level of students in this basic English IV class, Halaw felt that they needed direction in their assignments. For example, after students had read Act I of *The Glass Menagerie*, Andre had them read an excerpt from Tim O'Brien's *The Things They Carried*. The excerpt included the description of a pebble that one of the lieutenants carried as a good luck charm.

Halaw asked students to write an essay comparing what the glass menagerie symbolizes to one character in the play to what the pebble symbolizes to Lieutenant Jimmy Cross. Anabell noted: "The glass menagerie related to Laura because she is fragile. The glass menagerie is important to her, and she tries to preserve it because it stands for her perfect world. The pebble his girlfriend gave Jimmy Cross is important because it stands for their love." Frankie agreed that "Jim's 'glass menagerie' is the pebble he received from Martha. Since he received this pebble, he spent a lot of time in the war thinking about being with Martha at the Jersey shore. He devoted all free thought to the woman this pebble represented. If he lost it, he would be miserable." Anabell and Frankie both recognized the significance of a physical object to these different characters.

By having students first identify the significance of the objects in both stories on their own, Halaw was then able to introduce the concept of symbolism in a way that students could comprehend. These students might not have been able to grasp the significance of the symbol of the glass animals in the Williams' play without this intertextual connection. By first introducing a symbol in a context that they could comprehend—the separation of young lovers—Halaw was able to help these readers make the connection to a play that contained more abstract levels of symbolism.

As the study of *The Glass Menagerie* continued, Halaw showed the class a video of Williams' life entitled *Tennessee Williams: Orpheus of the American Stage.* They discussed Williams' life and identified major influences on it. Students, for example, noted the absence of a father and the responsibilities Williams felt for his mother and depressed sister. Viewing the video text led students to reconsider what they had read. As one student stated: "Laura became more real." By introducing the filmed interview visual text, Halaw was able to present background information in a way that cannot be done through lecture or class discussion.

After reading *The Glass Menagerie*, the students read *A Streetcar Named Desire*. Halaw then created an assignment to promote inter-textual thinking between the Williams' plays. While the class was studying *A Streetcar Named Desire*, Halaw gave them the following quotation from the opening of *The Glass Menagerie* and asked, "Which character from *A Streetcar Named Desire* would say this?"

I have tricks in my pocket; I have things up my sleeve. But I am the opposite of a stage magician. He gives you illusion that has the appearance of truth. I give you truth in the pleasant disguise of illusion.

Most of the students identified Blanche as the character who would say this because "she hides the truth with lies. . . . Like a stage magician she fools you." Two students, however, identified

Stanley as the person who would say this because, as Alan stated, "of the 'tricks' that he plays against Blanche. His truth is his anger." Alan's response and the discussion that followed show the power of intertextual connections. The word "tricks" in the quotation from *The Glass Menagerie* triggered a connection between the two texts. It helped Alan recognize Stanley's treatment of Blanche in a new way. He saw Stanley as always trying to "trick" Blanche into speaking the truth.

Other students' responses led to a discussion of the similarities in characters and themes between the two plays. This discussion led students to connect Blanche to Tom and then to Williams himself. Students saw all three people as creating illusions, of not letting the real world know them. Identifying commonalities that appear in both plays as well as in Williams' life helped the students come to their own understanding of themes and characters in this author's work.

After the students had read both Williams' plays, Halaw encouraged them to look for additional comparisons. Many students saw a connection among the characters. Brent explained that "Blanche resembles Laura from *The Glass Menagerie* because they both hide from the truth." Greg found that Blanche resembles Laura because "they both are considered outcasts from the people around them."

Other students made connections between Williams' plays and his life. Alan observed that "Blanche and Laura are both very close to their creator, Tennessee Williams. Together they represent his sister and him. Blanche is crazy like his sister. Laura is like both Williams and his sister. She needed help like Williams' sister and needed a father like him." Steve noticed that "Tom in *The Glass Menagerie* leaves to join the Merchant Marines. Williams wanted to travel the world. Also, Tom is the real name of Tennessee Williams." Greg observed the similarities between Blanche and Williams' sister—

"They were both placed in a mental ward." These and observations by other classmates were the basis for a class discussion in which the students explored the characters in both of the plays in depth. During the discussion, students noted that understanding Williams' life gave a "whole new meaning to the characters in the play."

The sophisticated level of the discussion in this class would not have been possible if they had read only one text by Williams. By reading the plays in tandem, students were better able to understand character motivation and development. When a characteristic such as "cruelty" was noted in one play, it led the students to consider a character from the other play. For example, during a class discussion of *A Streetcar Named Desire*, one boy mentioned the cruelty of Stanley. This observation led a classmate to comment that in *The Glass Menagerie* Tom was also cruel but not "in so straightforward a way." This helped the class see Tom in a new light—as a person who could be cruel in a passive way.

Near the end of the author study of Tennessee Williams, Halaw wanted to help his students see the connection between the author's intent and readers' reactions to his works. He introduced the concept through an author already familiar to the students, Stephen King. At the beginning of class, Halaw asked his students to respond to the following prompts in their journals: Why do people watch horror movies? Why do people write horror movies? Commenting on why people watch horror movies, the students responded "for the thrill," "as a stress outlet," "to get an adrenaline rush like a roller coaster," and "to test your fear." After sharing their responses, students read an essay, "Why We Crave Horror Movies" by Stephen King (2002), and then compared their journal entries to what King said in his essay. They were pleased to see that some of their ideas were directly reflected in King's essay, including the "roller coaster."

Halaw next asked them to think about why someone would write a horror story. The students' discussion led them to the conclusion that the author writes them for himself or herself not just for the reader or viewer. This was a revelation for some students in the class. As Frankie stated, "I never thought about how it is for the author himself before. They need to get their own dark emotions down."

Following the class discussion of King's essay, Halaw distributed an unidentified poem, "Life Story." Working in small groups, students read the poem to determine its message and to consider why a person would write a poem such as this. The class came to the consensus that the poem was "about a man who is dissatisfied." Oscar noted that the "man does not connect with other people. He and his lover are like two negative magnets pushing each away." Frankie added that "people only care about themselves." After the groups shared their ideas with the whole class, Halaw asked students whether they could identify who wrote the poem. A student said the author was Tennessee Williams.

Halaw then asked the class, "Based on what you know about him and his work, why would Tennessee Williams write this poem?" Maria observed that "Laura never really connected with anyone, and when she did, it all went wrong." Alan summed it up: "He was like Laura and Blanche. But he was crippled emotionally not physically. They were all crippled emotionally. He did not like himself." This observation led to a further discussion of the two Williams' plays the class had read. Some students compared Williams to both Tom in *The Glass Menagerie* and Blanche in *A Streetcar Named Desire*. Others compared him to Laura in *The Glass Menagerie* and to Blanche. Alan expressed his belief that "Williams really wanted to be Stanley from *Streetcar*, but he wasn't." Connecting to the earlier discussion in class, Oscar said, "He's writing it so he doesn't behave like that."

Because these students read two plays by Williams and studied his life, they were able to make sophisticated observations by connecting their prior reading to a new text—the "Life Story" poem. The intertextual nature of the unit made this possible. Halaw noted that students of this reading ability would not have comprehended *The Glass Menagerie* at the level this class did if they had not read the other works by Williams and made intertextual links. "The play [*Menagerie*] is too abstract for them if it is read alone," he observed.

> I was pleasantly surprised with the students' positive reception of the two plays. I will definitely teach Williams' works as an author study again. When we were reading *Streetcar*, the students referred back to *Menagerie* and compared the characters to both the play and Williams' own life. Their observations showed an understanding of common threads in Williams' works. They were able to see the effects of illusions on people's lives.

A final activity for the author study unit had intertextuality built directly into the assignment. Halaw divided the class into groups of three and asked each group to write a scripted conversation for three characters. One of the characters had to be from *The Glass Menagerie*, one had to be from *A Streetcar Named Desire*, and one had to be Tennessee Williams. The scripted conversations the students wrote and enacted demonstrated their understanding of the characters in both plays and how these characters have something in common with the author and each other (see Figure 6–2). The intertextual nature of the assignment encouraged students to stretch their thinking to connect the three characters in a new way.

Halaw was challenging these reluctant readers to think beyond a single text and make connections between works and between works and the author's life. The intertextual author study provided students with a context into which they could place the texts they were reading. It helped these basic English IV students comprehend the plays by connecting them to the author's life and to each other.

Figure 6–2

"Playtime Crossover" by Alan W.

(The setting is in Tennessee Williams' home, a friend has informed a friend of his own of Tennessee, and that he is a person worth meeting. The friend's friend feels otherwise, but goes to see why Tennessee's friend thinks this about him. His girlfriend accompanies him.)

TENNESSEE: So . . . you know a friend of mine?

STANLEY: Yea, said you're an "interesting" character.

TENNESSEE: Hmm, I'm probably not that interesting unless you know me well.

STANLEY: I usually figure people out pretty quick; you don't seem like the joyous type, friend said you was a writer.

TENNESSEE: Yes, I did write some plays . . .

STANLEY: I don't read much, but it seems like you'd write happy plays.

TENNESSEE: I write what I know . . . would you like a drink? I'm going to the kitchen to get one.

STANLEY: Yea, got any Southern Comfort?

TENNESSEE: I believe so, yes . . . what did you say your name was again?

STANLEY: Stan, why ya askin'?

TENNESSEE: I know a man like you, it's quite strange . . .

(Tennessee goes into the kitchen. While he is occupied, a knock is heard at the door. Stanley answers it.)

STANLEY: Well it's about time you got here! You're ten minutes late!

AMANDA: I'm quite sorry. I saw quite the man on the way here, dressed up in a suit! I wonder where he could be going in such an outfit?

STANLEY: I'm your boyfriend you shouldn't be lookin' at other guys! Why are you like that anyway, you crazy dame? I'm better than those guys.

AMANDA: There's no problem in just lookin' deary! I just enjoyed seeing the man in a suit; I wouldn't mind seeing you in one more either.

STANLEY: You know I ain't like that Amanda, not my thing.

TENNESSEE: *(Calling from the kitchen.)* Is there someone else in there Stanley?

STANLEY: Yea! My girlfriend Amanda.

continued on next page

Figure 6–2 *continued from previous page*

TENNESSEE: You don't say! Another coincidence, I know someone just like her from what I've heard; quite the odd happening . . .

(Tennessee comes out from the kitchen and brings a drink for Stanley and himself.)

TENNESSEE: I'm afraid I don't have much for you on such short notice Miss Amanda. I wasn't informed beforehand . . .

AMANDA: Oh it's OK . . . I'll suffice without it I suppose. Stanley! Don't drink like such an ill-mannered man!

STANLEY: I'll drink however I want to! You ain't the boss of me!

TENNESSEE: You two date?

STANLEY: Oh yea all the time; she's my lady. Ain't that right Amanda?

AMANDA: Oh my, yes it is.

TENNESSEE: Well now, I see it. I'm quite familiar with this kind of relationship.

STANLEY: You had one?

TENNESSEE: You could say that . . .

STANLEY: You're an odd fellow you know that? You're hiding something and making it seem kind of obvious, not on purpose though. It seems set in with you, ya know that? At least with Amanda and me it's obvious and we ain't hiding anything. We ain't bottled up inside and angry at each other. Amanda is an overbearing woman at times, but I've gotten used to it and showed her what's what . . . What's said is said and we move on. Thing is you oughta just tell your problem, ya know? I'm pretty sure we gotta get going anyway. Come on Amanda, it's bowling night.

AMANDA: Yes deary, comin'!

(They walk out, and Tennessee sits in silence for several minutes mulling over what Stanley said, and the two visitors' resemblances to his own characters.)

TENNESSEE: Bye then . . .

English IV—Peer input by:

Frankie C.

Sean F.

Anthony R.

Making Connections:
Archetypes

7

The concept of archetypes in literary criticism is closely linked to the work of the philosopher Carl Jung who believed that people carry, deep within themselves, memories of a common past, of experiences shared by all human beings. He called this shared memory the "collective unconscious" and saw this collective unconscious reflected in the archetypes that appear around us. Jung defined an *archetype* as "a universal and recurring image, pattern, or motif representing a typical human experience" (Hero's Quest Website, 2004). In his book, *The Hero with a Thousand Faces,* Joseph Campbell (1971) applied the work of Jung to myths and other literary texts. Campbell noted that images, plots, symbols, and characters that exist in the collective unconscious are brought to light in literary works that span cultures and time. The hero, the flood, the trickster, the serpent, the outcast, the river, the wise old man, and the quest are but a few of the recurring universal archetypes found in literature and other texts.

Because archetypes are universal, they provide a powerful tool for making connections among texts. Recurring character types, images, plots, motifs, and symbols provide links that a reader can trace from one text to another. The hero's quest is one of the most widely read and most frequently taught archetypes in literature. The quest motif can be found in works ranging from the Indian epic *Mahabharata*, compiled between 200 B.C. and 200 A.D.E., and the *Harry Potter* films. Dorothy's journey in the *Wizard of Oz* is an example of the same universal quest that Odysseus made on his journey home from the Trojan War. The hero's journey can be both a physical and a spiritual one, an outward and an inward journey of discovery.

The Hero's Quest

The quest motif is frequently represented in the form of a hero's quest. Stories that contain a hero's quest generally include a journey that follows three phases: a call or summons, the confrontation of hardships, and the return home. In addition to these phases, individual hero quests include similar characteristics within the journey. The hero's quest model and its traits identified in this chapter are based on the work of Joseph Campbell as presented in Peter Stillman's book, *Introduction to Myth* (1985, 36–41).

Using the Stillman model, an intertextual study of the hero's quest based on the following works of literature is presented here:

- The Sumerian epic *Gilgamesh*

- The Greek tragedy *Oedipus Rex* by Sophocles

- Two modern works: *Their Eyes Were Watching God* by Zora Neale Hurston and the American short story "A Worn Path" by Eudora Welty

- The American novel *The Great Gatsby* by F. Scott Fitzgerald

Although these works represent different genres, the model presented in this chapter focuses on archetype as the common thread for intertextual study, rather than the texts' structure. Each of the stories included in this unit contains the elements of the hero's quest as defined by Stillman. Examples of the elements follow; classroom examples for each of the elements are presented in Appendix E.

1. Heroes are often of obscure or mysterious origins.

2. Heroes are neither fools nor invincible.

3. The hero's way isn't always direct or clear for him or her.

4. The hero has a goal.

5. The hero's way is beset with dangers, loneliness, and temptation.

6. Frequently, friends, servants, or disciples accompany the hero.

7. The hero has a guide or guides.

8. The hero descends into darkness.

9. The hero is not the same after emerging from the darkness of his or her descent.

10. What the hero seeks is usually no more than a symbol of what he or she really finds.

11. The hero suffers a wound.

12. Mythological heroes tend to be males.

In teaching the hero's quest, we have added to Stillman's list the following characteristic found in Campbell's original work:

13. Frequently, the hero returns to the everyday world to share his or her knowledge with others or to bring to consciousness new and better ways of living.

Teaching the Hero's Quest

Seniors in all levels of senior English at South Brunswick High School study the archetype of the quest. Zandrea Eagle teaches a unit on this archetype to both basic and college preparatory English students successfully. Her unit begins with an inductive approach to teaching the hero's quest. While reading the short story "A Worn Path," students are asked to identify characteristics of heroes and the hero's quest before they are are introduced to the Stillman model; that is, they are not given the unit's essential questions until after they have read the first short story.

Eudora Welty's "A Worn Path" is used as an introduction to exemplify the elements of the quest motif. Before reading the short story for homework, however, students in Eagle's English class were asked to brainstorm, first with partners and then as a whole class, about what makes a hero a hero. They constructed a list that reflects some of the traits identified by Campbell and Stillman: a hero is brave, is larger than life, accomplishes something superhuman, conquers a fear or an enemy, helps others. Because this is a prereading list, students' answers were not judged right or wrong or elaborated on. The teacher then assigned the short story "A Worn Path" and instructed the class to keep their list in mind as they read.

The next time the class met, the list they constructed previously was posted and Eagle asked students whether, based on the story they had just read, they now wanted to add anything. The list of a hero's traits was expanded as students added: the hero helps someone else, leaves home, faces many dangers or problems, and can be a woman. After they revised their list, Eagle introduced the characteristics of a hero's quest as outlined in Stillman's book so that students could compare them (Figure 7–1).

After discussing the similarities and differences, Eagle divided the students into small groups and asked them to revisit "A Worn

Figure 7–1

Elements of the Hero's Quest

Class List for a Hero	Stillman's List for a Hero
leaves home	is of mysterious origins
is brave	is neither a fool nor invincible
is larger than life	his way is not always clear
accomplishes something	has a goal
superhuman	his way is beset with dangers,
conquers a fear or an enemy	loneliness, and temptation
faces many dangers or problems	is often accompanied by a
helps someone else	friend or companion
can be a woman	has a guide or guides
helps others	descends into darkness
	seeks no more than a symbol
	of what he finds
	suffers a wound
	mythological heroes tend to
	be male

Path" and to identify as many of the characteristics on Stillman's list as they could. It should be noted that the students had a copy of the Welty story separate from the Stillman book so that his identification of the elements did not affect their analysis. Each group was able to complete this task. The students seemed amazed by how neatly the story fit the model. Comments such as, " way cool" and "I had no idea" were overheard as each group worked.

Next, students were given the essential questions for the unit (Figure 7–2); they were also posted on the classroom wall. During a class discussion, students offered answers to some of the questions based on the short story they had read. The teacher reminded them

Making Connections: Archetypes

Figure 7–2

Planning Intertextual Studies: The Quest Archetype

Course: English IV

Unit: The Quest Motif

Texts:

Gilgamesh (Sumerian epic)

Oedipus by Sophocles (drama)

Their Eyes Were Watching God by Zora Neale Hurston (novel)

"A Worn Path" by Eudora Welty (short story)

The Great Gatsby by F. Scott Fitzgerald (novel)

Form of Intertextual Study: Archetype

Purpose:

To help students understand the universality of archetypes.

To help students understand the enduring importance of the quest motif in literature.

To help students understand how the same motif can be represented in diverse cultures and in different times.

Essential Questions:

How does a society define a hero?

What makes the hero's quest endure?

How does society's view of a hero's quest change over time?

How does a classical hero's quest differ from a modern hero's quest?

How are male and female quests the same?

How are male and female quests different?

Unit Questions:

What is a quest?

What is an archetype?

How is a quest an archetype?

What are some of the different forms a quest can take?

What are the elements of a hero's quest?

continued on next page

Figure 7–2 *continued from previous page*

How is each work we read an example of a hero's quest?

How are the works the same? How are they different?

In what ways are the main characters the same?

Assessments:

Literary analysis essay comparing two or more core texts, focusing on their interpretations of the quest motif

Open-ended timed writing applying the quest motif to a work read outside of class

Short quizzes to check for understanding

Socratic Seminar class discussions

Performance Assessment:

As a member of the editorial staff at a textbook company, you have been asked to write an introduction for an anthology of literary works that centers around the quest motif. Your audience consists of high school teachers and students. Your goal is to help them understand why your company included the texts they did for this anthology.

Learning Activities:

Students read the short story "A Worn Path" and, working in small groups, identify the elements of the hero's quest in the story.

Students keep reader response journals and make entries for each of the texts read. Students can use their journals for reference during class discussions and when writing their essays.

Students complete a Venn diagram comparing two texts from different periods and/or cultures that contain archetypes.

Students research the authors and/or time periods in which each of the core texts was written. This may be done as a "jigsaw" activity with different groups of students researching different authors and/or time periods.

Differentiated Activities

Advanced students: Research the concept of the feminine hero's quest and prepare an oral report for the class.

Reluctant readers: Complete a comparison chart identifying elements of the hero's quest in one of the texts studied and in a movie you have seen.

that they would be returning to these essential questions throughout the unit, and that they could change or elaborate on their answers as the unit progressed. Eagle then presented an overview of the other works students would be reading: *Gilgamesh* and *Oedipus Rex;* this class had read *Their Eyes Were Watching God* the previous year. Students were instructed to keep reader response journals as they read and to keep reviewing the essential questions. *Gilgamesh* was assigned as the next text to read.

After each of the core works was read, students participated in a discussion in the form of a Socratic Seminar on archetypes. A Socratic Seminar is a true discussion in which, sitting in a circle, the students talk directly to each other, raising and answering questions and sharing observations. During these discussions students began making more and more links to the texts previously read. The majority of the connections made focused on the main characters or characteristics of the hero's quest. As one student noted: "Now whenever I finish a novel, I find myself thinking if it is a hero's quest." Another student added: "Knowing the hero's quest helps me understand literature and film better. The fact that many characters fit the hero archetype helps me to understand the character a whole lot better." As one student, Robin, noted: " I now see that a hero's quest can be internal and not just a journey. This helped me see how Janie and Phoenix are more like Gilgamesh than I thought. Actually, I would not have thought about this if I hadn't read them both this way."

Another senior English teacher, Andy Loh, reviewed the hero's quest with his students near the end of the school year, encouraging them to reflect on all the texts they had studied, including print texts and films. As Jason observed, "It really explains why all heroes have to take an eventual fall. In movies it can be quite discouraging to constantly see the good guys have a great loss, but it's all part of the hero's quest." A second student in Loh's class noted how understanding the hero's quest helped her: "Now, instead of just reading for plot, climax, and those sort of things, I can now read more in depth." When asked what she meant by this, she added, "I can see patterns and look for relationships, you know, connections." Another classmate, Beth, put it differently: "It [the hero's quest] has helped me define what a hero is and think of past heroes."

Several students commented on how studying the archetype of the hero's quest helped them better understand and connect works of literature. As Keneisha stated: "*Hamlet* has helped my understanding of literature because it showed me similarities within tragedies. I never realized that literature had similar characteristics." Another girl, Sydnee, made a connection to *Their Eyes Were Watching God*:

> You can apply it [a hero's quest] to Janie's part in *Their Eyes Were Watching God* because of her struggle as a woman trying to find someone who would love her as much as she would love them. When she keeps trying to find a man, she falls into the darkness and emerges stronger, always on her quest to find something to complete her life.

Kyle added, "I realize that you can teach the same lesson through a variety of different stories." This student went on to compare the core literary works the class read to *Star Wars* and *Lord of the Rings*.

English teacher Yoshi Lassiter and Special Education teacher Stacy Svare cotaught a senior inclusion basic English class, which included a number of students classified as "unmotivated." They had read *Their Eyes Were Watching God* in their junior year and *Oedipus Rex* and *Siddhartha* in the senior year. During a class discussion of the quest archetype, one reluctant reader, Gerard, noted that, "understanding the hero's quest makes the story worth checking out." A classmate added: "Now I get it. Oedipus is like Siddhartha. They are both looking for something and get into trouble trying to find it. Just like we all do." This student realized the universality of the quest archetype, how it cuts across time and place because it applies to all people. The comments these students made indicated that they were thinking about what they had read and making connections among the texts. While making connections, they also were developing a better understanding of the messages presented in the readings being compared.

In addition to the core works studied as a class, each marking period students at South Brunswick High School read an outside text of their own choosing. For the marking period during which the hero's quest was studied, teachers gave students a list of works from which they were to select an outside reading text. The list included *Siddhartha*, *The Great Gatsby*, *The Awakening*, *Idylls of the King*, and *Beowulf; The Odyssey* was not included because they had studied it during their freshman year. Eagle offered her students the choice of focusing on the female quest story by reading *Antigone* by Sophocles, *Their Eyes Were Watching God* by Zora Neale Hurston, *Gilgamesh: A Novel* by the Australian author Joan London, or three briefer works as one selection—*The Yellow Wallpaper* by Charlotte Perkins, *The Story of an Hour* by Kate Chopin, and *The Awakening* by Kate Chopin.

In the spring of their senior year, all students at South Brunswick High School view and study Mike Nichols' film, *The Graduate*. As the class discussed the film, students, without teacher prompting, began making connections to the quest motif they had been studying all year. In Doris Bacon's senior English class, Imani stated: "*The Graduate* is a quest because the main character, Ben, doesn't know who he [is] and his quest is to find it out, to discover the purpose he has in life." A classmate, Sean, added: "Ben must descend into emotional despair. He gives in to his loneliness, his darkness when he sleeps with Mrs. Robinson." In his reflection at the end of the year, Sean added: "Understanding the hero's quest has broadened my understanding of literature and film. I can see that heroes are a lot like ordinary people, and now I can relate to the characters' situations more." Gayle noted: "I can never read a book or look at a movie the same way again." Gayle's sentiments were echoed by a number of students. Having studied the hero's quest, they developed schemata against which to measure future texts. This was shown in the reflection of a struggling reader who said, "After understanding the concept of a hero's quest, it becomes a lot easier to understand many works of big authors." His classmate concluded: "Now I must go on a hero's quest myself!"

The students' understanding of the common elements of a hero's quest helps them when reading or viewing a new text. When watching *Star Wars*, for example, students were realizing a deeper meaning than the surface adventure story when they recognized the archetype of the hero's quest. Many of the reluctant readers in Lassiter's and Svare's classes were also able to connect the archetypes in the hero's quest to films they had seen, including *The Lion King, Harry Potter*, and *Finding Nemo*. Understanding the different elements of the hero's quest not only helped students understand the stories studied in class in a new way, but also helped them reexamine texts outside of the classroom in a new light.

The quest motif provides the basis for an intertextual study in the classroom that can be as limited or as far-reaching as time, interest, and the curriculum permit. Additional suggested works that can be included in an intertextual study based on the hero's quest are listed in this book's Appendix B.

The students and teachers described in this book engaged in purposeful intertextual studies. The teachers modeled reading behaviors that support intertexual thought and gave their students the tools to do so. The teachers were often surprised and always impressed with the connections their students made and the depth of understanding these connections revealed. After several months of using an intertextual approach to literature, these teachers noted that the students "made it their own." All the teacher now needed to say is "think about connections," and the students are "off and running." This is the goal of all teachers—to make their students independent thinkers and learners. This is what happens when text meets text.

Appendix A: Intertextual Response Journal Assignment for *Hamlet*

Developed by April Gonzalez

1. Keep a journal for each act in *Hamlet*. The journal responses will be used for class discussions and writing assignments. Entries for each act will be graded as a homework assignment.
2. Include three (3) connections to previous knowledge or prior reading that helps you understand the passages you identify in your journal. Explain the intertextual connection clearly.
3. Write three (3) questions you have about each act and be prepared to share the questions with the class.

Appendix B:
Paired Texts

Core Text	Paired Text(s)	Connections
Kim by Rudyard Kipling	*The Game* by Laurie King	characters, setting, genre (suspense story)
Mrs. Dalloway by Virginia Woolf	*The Hours* by Michael Cunningham *To the Lighthouse* by Virginia Woolf	theme, characters, archetypes author, theme
Ariel by Sylvia Plath	*Wintering* by Kate Moses *The Bell Jar* by Sylvia Plath	genre, theme, plot, author
Moby-Dick by Herman Melville	*In the Heart of the Sea* by Nathaniel Philbrick "In Cabin'd Ships at Sea" by Walt Whitman	theme, genre
Passing by Neela Larsen	*Imitation of Life* (film) *Black Like Me* by John Howard Griffin	media, theme
The Crucible by Arthur Miller	*Salem Falls* by Jodi Picoult *The Scarlet Letter* by Nathaniel Hawthorne *Tituba* by Alyssa Barillari	theme, genre theme, setting, plot, characters theme, setting, plot, characters, archetypes

Core Text	Paired Text(s)	Connections
Romeo and Juliet by William Shakespeare	"The Tragical History of Romeus and Juliet" poem by Arthur Brooke	genre
	West Side Story by Arthur Laurents Leonard Bernstein's and Stephen Sondheim's music for *Romeo and Juliet*	media, theme, characters, plot, archetypes
	Franco Zefirelli's *Romeo and Juliet* (film)	
	Baz Luhrmann's *Romeo and Juliet* (film)	
	Ballet music*: Sergei Prokofiev*	
Hamlet by William Shakespeare	"Amleth" from Saxo Grammaticus' *History of Denmark (Historicae Danicae)*	characters, setting, plot, theme, genre (revenge tragedy)
	The Spanish Tragedy by Thomas Kyd	archetypes
	Rosencrantz and Guildenstern Are Dead by Thomas Stoppard	theme, character
	Titus Andronicus by William Shakespeare	author, genre (revenge tragedy)
	Films:	
	Lawrence Olivier's *Hamlet*	media, archetypes, plot, characters, setting
	Kenneth Branaugh's *Hamlet*	
	Mel Gibson's *Hamlet*	
	Stephen Mills' *Hamlet,* the ballet	genre
		archetypes (quest motif), genre
King Lear by William Shakespeare	*The Poetics* by Aristotle	archetypes (tragic hero)
	Death of a Salesman by Arthur Miller	
	Oedipus Rex by Sophocles	
	Medea by Euripedes	
	Othello by William Shakespeare	
	Macbeth by William Shakespeare	
	Hamlet by William Shakespeare	
Macbeth by William Shakespeare	Holinshed's *Chronicles of England, Scotland, and Ireland*	themes, characters, setting, plot, archetypes
	The Third Witch by Rebecca Reisert	theme, character, plot
	The Chocolate War by Robert Cormier	theme, character, genre
	Films:	
	Akira Kurosawa's *Throne of Blood*	media, themes, archetypes
	Orson Welles' *Macbeth*	

Core Text	Paired Text(s)	Connections
Their Eyes Were Watching God by Zora Neale Hurston	*So Long a Letter* by Mariama Ba	theme, archetypes, characters
	To the Lighthouse by Virginia Woolf	
	Mrs. Dalloway by Virginia Woolf	
	A Room of One's Own by Virginia Woolf	
	The Awakening by Kate Chopin	
	"The Yellow Wallpaper" by Charlotte Perkins Stetson Gilman	theme, genre
	Wife by Bharati Mukherjee	theme
	The Color Purple by Alice Walker	theme
	In Search of Our Mothers' Gardens, by Alice Walker	theme, genre
The Canterbury Tales by Geoffrey Chaucer	*The River Sutra* by Gita Mehta	genre, plot, theme
Heart of Darkness by Joseph Conrad	*Things Fall Apart* by Chinua Achebe	theme, setting
	The Secret Sharer by Joseph Conrad	author, theme
	Film:	
	Apocalypse Now	
Things Fall Apart by Chinua Achebe	*Kaffir Boy* by Mark Mathabane	theme, setting
	Cry, the Beloved Country by Alan Paton	
	"The Second Coming" poem by W. B. Yeats	theme, genre
	Film:	
	The Power of One	theme, setting
Jane Eyre by Charlotte Bronte	*The Wide Sargasso Sea* by Jean Rhys	character, theme, plot
Girl with a Pearl Earring by Tracy Chevalier	*Girl with a Pearl Earring* painting by Johannes Vermeer	genre, theme
The Grapes of Wrath by John Steinbeck	*Of Mice and Men* by John Steinbeck	author, theme, archetype, setting
	Steinbeck's play version: *Of Mice and Men*	genre, author
	Dust on the Tracks by Karen Hess	theme, genre, setting

Core Text	Paired Text(s)	Connections
A Raisin in the Sun by Lorraine Hansberry	"Harlem" by Langston Hughes	genre, theme
	To Be Young Gifted and Black by Lorraine Hansberry	theme, author
	The Great Migration by Walter Dean Myers	genre, theme
	Artwork:	
	The Great Migration by Jacob Lawrence	
	The Glory Field by Walter Dean Myers	
	Films:	
	A Raisin in the Sun, starring Sydney Poitier	character, plot, theme
	A Raisin in the Sun, starring Danny Glover	
Oedipus Rex by Sophocles	*The Epic of Gilgamesh* (Sumerian)	genre, archetype
	The Mahabharata, Indian Epic (excerpts)	archetypes (quest motif), genre, themes
	The Odyssey by Homer	
	Le Morte D'Arthur by Thomas Mallory	
	Idylls of the King by Alfred Lord Tennyson	
	Perceval by Chretien de Troyes	
	Don Quixote by Miguel de Cervantes	
	Moby-Dick by Herman Melville	
	Siddhartha by Hermann Hesse	
	Their Eyes Were Watching God by Zora Neale Hurston	
	The Adventures of Huckleberry Finn by Mark Twain	
	The Lord of the Rings by J.R.R. Tolkien	
	"A Worn Path" by Eudora Welty	
	"Tell all the truth, but tell it slant" poem by Emily Dickinson	
	"Oedipus" poem by Josephine Mills	
	Harry Potter series by J. K. Rowlings	
	Films:	
	Star Wars series	
	Lord of the Rings series	
	The Matrix series	
	Harry Potter series	
	The Wizard of Oz	

Core Text	Paired Text(s)	Connections
A Catcher in the Rye by J. D. Salinger	*A Separate Peace* by John Knowles	theme, archetype (coming of age)
	The Adventures of Huckleberry Finn by Mark Twain	
	Their Eyes Were Watching God by Zora Neale Hurston	
	Ethan Frome by Edith Warton	
	The Red Badge of Courage by Stephen Crane	
	Lord of the Flies by William Golding	
	To Kill a Mockingbird by Harper Lee	
	Old Yeller by Fred Gibson	
	A Member of the Wedding by Carson McCullers	
	Sing Down the Moon by Scott O'Dell	
	Things Fall Apart by Chinua Achebe	
	Kaffir Boy by Mark Mathabane	genre, theme
	Incidents in the Life of a Slave Girl by Harriet Jacobs	genre, interdisciplinary
	Lucy by Jamaica Kincaid	
	Running in the Family by Michael Ondaatje	
	Coming of Age in Mississippi by Anne Moody	
	Brighton Beach Memoirs by Neil Simon	
	Nine Stories by J. D. Salinger	
	Reviving Ophelia: Saving the Selves of Adolescent Girls by Mary Pipher	

When Text Meets Text

Appendix C: Bringing It All Together: A Study of Chinua Achebe's *Things Fall Apart*

A unit designed for use in the Grade 12 Curriculum of South Brunswick High School
By April Gonzalez, Barbara King-Shaver, Andy Loh

Text:

Things Fall Apart, Chinua Achebe

Resources:

The Abolition of Man, C. S. Lewis—nonfiction

"The Second Coming," William Butler Yeats—poem

The Holy Bible (specifically Matthew 24 and Revelation 13)

www.scholars.nus.edu.sg/landow/post/achebe/achebeov.html—Chinua Achebe/African culture page with plentiful information

www.wsu.edu:8000/~brians/anglophone/achebe.html—*Things Fall Apart* Study Guide

www.unesco.org/courier/2001_06/uk/dires.htm—Interview with Achebe

Enduring Understandings:

- The archetypes of the hero and the tragic hero are evident in multiple works of literature.
- A person needs to come to his or her own understanding of his or her identity apart from external influences.
- Morality is both culturally and universally defined.
- Cultural expectations of the roles of men and women often lead to conflict.
- When a culture's tradition is challenged, change is inevitable.
- The father–son relationship plays a role in the formation of the next generation.

Essential Questions:

- How is the concept of a hero universal, yet culturally defined?
- What are the dangers involved in living one's life as a reaction to the models and expectations of others?

- Is there such a thing as universally binding morality or is all morality culturally conditioned and dependent on society?
- Does society prescribe the roles of men and women or is there such a thing as inherent masculinity and femininity?
- What role does tradition play in sustaining a culture and/or society?
- What is the nature of the father–son relationship, and how does it impact the individual?

Unit Questions:
- How does or doesn't Okonkwo fit the archetype of the tragic hero?
- Why does Achebe use a line from "The Second Coming" as a title for the novel?
- How does the poem connect to the themes of the novel?
- What roles do proverbs, folklore, religion, and superstition play in the novel?
- What are the religious, social, and moral issues caused by the clash of cultures in the novel?
- How does the author use irony to get his point across?
- How are the decisions Okonkwo makes affected by his relationships to his father and his son?
- What is the role of women in the novel, and what is Achebe's attitude regarding this?
- How does Achebe's style support meaning within the chapters and throughout the novel?
- What is the role of the elderly wise man? Is this role limited to the Ibo society?

Students will know:
- the plot, theme, and characters of *Things Fall Apart*.
- the biography and works of Chinua Achebe.
- African and American proverbs.
- the geography of Africa.
- the history of Colonialism in Africa.

Students will be able to:
- participate in a Socratic Seminar.
- explain theme in the novel.
- explain the impact of colonialism on Africans.

When Text Meets Text

- present an oral report.
- work individually and in cooperative groups.
- read the novel out loud and silently.

Integrated Skills:
- Students will engage in reading, writing, speaking, and listening during this unit.

Performance Assessment and Rubric:
- *Proverbs in the World*—You are a writer for *The Multicultural Review*.

  The magazine is interested in publishing a thematic issue on the universality of proverbs. You have been assigned to research and find commonalities between the African proverbs cited in *Things Fall Apart* and the cultures of the rest of the world. After you complete your research, you will submit an article to the magazine.

Other Assessments:
- Multiple-choice test
- Timed writing
- Oral report
- Socratic Seminar/class discussion

Suggested Learning Activities:

Prereading Activity

"The Second Coming" poem—Each student will be presented with an index card on which there is one of six quotations from the Bible. Students will assemble into six groups according to those who have the same quotation. In these groups, students will be asked to try to determine where the quote comes from. If they have prior knowledge of the biblical allusion, they can elaborate in writing. If not, they will be asked to engage in creative writing and make up a story and/or context for the quotation. After five minutes, all groups will report to the class, then the instructor will hand out copies of the poem to the students and read it out loud twice.

Using students' prior knowledge, the class will piece together the historical and literary allusions to Christ's First and Second Comings in order to prepare students for the context of the poem. Students will read the poem silently again and take five minutes to analyze it in their groups. Each group then presents its findings to the class. After this, students will read the chapters in the Bible from which the quotations are taken and discuss the poem's meaning as a class. Students will then speculate on the novel's plot.

Vocabulary

ominous	oracle	effeminate	impotent
adherents	zeal	ostracize	wherewithal
dispensation	desecrated	sacrilege	abomination
exacting	revered	malevolent	harbingers
atone	dynamism	resignation	inadvertent

Crosscultural Values

Small groups will be given a list of quotations, from various cultures, based on the same theme taken from the appendix of C. S. Lewis' *The Abolition of Man.*

Part I—Students will read the list and discuss how various cultures view the same topic.

Part II—Students will identify at least two quotations from *Things Fall Apart* that best represent the thematic idea. Explain how the quotations from the novel compare to those of other cultures.

Writing Assignment

Choose one of the following topics. Compose a rough draft and edit it with a peer. This is considered a process writing, so your rough draft, revisions, and final draft will be taken into account for your grade.

1. Compose an additional chapter exploring how Ezinma copes with her father's suicide. Add information about her upcoming marriage and the establishment of her family. Imagine what she will tell her children about their grandfather. You should model this chapter after Achebe. Note elements of style, the author's attitude, and the point of view of the novel.

2. Take a position on whether Okonkwo is a hero. Define what a hero is in your introduction. Then, using this definition, provide specific details and/or incidents from the novel to support your position. In your conclusion, refer to the definition provided in the introduction.

3. Discuss the effects on the Ibo tribe of the arrival of the white man. The effects may be emotional as well as physical. Consider the tradition and belief systems of the culture as you provide examples and specific details to support your points. In your conclusion, make a suggestion as to how the reader might apply the information presented in your essay.

A Nigerian Bill of Rights

Student Directions: The League of Nations (the forerunner of the United Nations) is sponsoring a peace summit between the leaders of Umuofia, members of the British Establishment, and the Ibo Christian leaders of Umuofia. All three groups will convene with the goal of developing a Nigerian Bill of Rights containing only ten articles that must serve at least some of the needs of each group. All three groups must ratify this document in order for it to become the rule of the land. As a leader of Umuofia, a member of the British Establishment, or an Ibo Christian, you attend the summit and represent your interests in an oral presentation.

Teacher Directions: Students will be assigned to one of three groups: Colonial, with the role of a missionary or government official; Ibo tribal leader, with the role of *egwugwu*, highest-titled noble, priest/priestess; or Ibo Christian, with interests in both societies.

Students will be given fifteen minutes to convene in their respective groups and discuss their own needs based on the novel and handouts about Nigerian history.

Each group will have to elect a spokesperson from among them to present its case. With the instructor or another student acting as chief diplomat, each group will present in five minutes or less. After the initial five-minute presentation, groups will be invited to respond and/or counterargue each position. Following the response period, spokespersons will rejoin their small groups to help develop a Nigerian Bill of Rights that incorporates the diverse interests of everyone.

Each group will then share its version with the other groups and come to a consensus on the proposals. The chief diplomat will then serve as Chairman of the General Assembly and try to get a Bill of Rights ratified that all groups will accept. A general vote would then be held on the final document; it needs to be ratified by two-thirds of the Assembly.

Note: Academic and Honors teachers might consider assigning each student a position paper from his or her perspective.

Appendix D: Selected Strategies That Support Intertextual Study

These activities include differentiated assignments based on students' readiness, interests, and learning styles.

Prereading

Teacher helps students access prior knowledge by brainstorming their knowledge of texts and/or issues to be studied.

Teacher helps students access prior knowledge by using a prereading checklist of key terms and concepts from the unit.

Teacher helps students access prior knowledge by completing a prereading graphic organizer.

During Reading

Students maintain a reading log of intertextual connections they make.

Students complete a double-entry log.

Students write questions they wish to discuss based on their readings.

Students share journal entries and class discussions are based on intertextual connections.

Students make marginal notes of connections they see as they read. These are done in the book or on sticky notes.

Postreading

Students participate in class discussions, literature circles, and Socratic Seminars on issues raised and intertextual connections.

Students conduct follow-up research on issues and connections raised.

Students suggest related works that could be included in this unit.

Students select a related work and read it independently, keeping a log of intertextual connections as they read.

Students compose a formal essay demonstrating their understanding of connections between or among the texts studied.

Students write a reflection on what they learned from the intertextual study.

Students assume the role of a character in one text and write a letter to a character in a paired text.

Students in the role of an author write a letter from the author of one text to the author of another.

Students complete a comparison chart or other graphic organizer of two or more works studied.

Appendix E: Elements of the Hero's Quest with Examples

1. *Heroes are often of obscure or mysterious origins.*

   In the Sumerian epic, Gilgamesh, the King of Uruk, is the offspring of a goddess mother and a mortal father. Oedipus, the title character in *Oedipus Rex*, did not know his true origins. Janie, the protagonist in *Their Eyes Were Watching God*, was raised by her grandmother, her mother being absent and her father being unknown. Phoenix, the grandmother in "A Worn Path," lives outside of town, and the townspeople know little about her. In fact, when the woman at the medical facility asks Phoenix for her history, she does not answer. Phoenix herself does not know how old she is. Having created his own past, Gatsby's true past is a secret.

2. *Heroes are neither fools nor invincible.*

   As Gilgamesh proceeds on his journey, the reader recognizes that there is more substance to Gilgamesh than the playboy king presented in the beginning of the epic. The reader also learns that Gilgamesh can be defeated as shown by the serpent near the end of the tale. By solving the riddle of the Sphinx, Oedipus shows that he is no fool. When he learns the truth of his parentage, the reader realizes that Oedipus is not invincible. In *Their Eyes Were Watching God*, Janie's quick actions during the flood are indications of her intelligence and common sense. However, when the men in her life hurt her repeatedly, the reader sees Janie's vulnerability. Similar to Janie in *Their Eyes Were Watching God*, Phoenix in "A Worn Path" is also shown to have common sense and innate intelligence even though she is an uneducated woman. Phoenix is physically fragile and capable of being harmed as shown during her fall into the ditch. Jay Gatsby is no fool. He has made money and followed a plan in his life, but he is also not invincible. Gatsby can be hurt by the woman he adores, and in the end, he dies for her.

3. *The hero's way isn't always direct or clear for him or her.*

   At the beginning of the epic, Gilgamesh believes his right is to rule Uruk as a tyrannical king. Oedipus believes he has escaped his fate when he moves to Thebes. As a young woman, Janie believes that if she marries an older, stable man, she will be happy. And Phoenix does not believe she will find anything more than medicine for her grandson when she journeys to town. Gatsby believes that Daisy is fine and good, but learns too late that she has faults like everyone else.

4. *The hero has a goal.*

    Gilgamesh begins his journey searching for one thing, the giant Humbaba, but his final quest is for eternal life. Oedipus searches for the cause of his city's troubles and the slayer of King Laius but actually finds his true identity. Janie begins her journey searching for the love of a man but ends it as an independent woman. Phoenix journeys to town to get medicine for her grandson, but she returns with an unexpected gift for him. Gatsby wants the woman behind that green light at the end of the dock—Daisy.

5. *The hero's way is beset with dangers, loneliness, and temptation.*

    When Gilgamesh loses his friend Enkidu to a mortal wound, he becomes despaired because of his loneliness. Gilgamesh then encounters many obstacles on his quest for eternal life, culminating with his struggle with the serpent. Oedipus must face the temptation of pride. He cares very much for his family and his city, but he ends up exiled and lonely. In *Their Eyes Were Watching God*, others, particularly the men around her, hurt Janie both emotionally and physically. In the end, Janie also must finish her journey alone. In "A Worn Path," Phoenix makes a solitary, difficult physical journey to Natchez. Having fallen and becoming confused, Phoenix gives in to temptation and keeps a lost nickel. On his journey to obtain wealth, Gatsby gets involved with shady characters and illegal dealings. He gives in to these temptations and he ends up as he started, alone.

6. *Frequently, the hero is accompanied by friends, servants, or disciples.*

    In many of the hero's tales, friends, servants, and disciples can also serve as guides. The two are intertwined in the stories studied here and are explained in number seven.

7. *The hero has a guide or guides.*

    Gilgamesh has several friends and guides along the way, including his best friend Enkidu, his mother, the goddess Ninsun, and the wise old man Utnapishtim. In the Greek tragedy, Oedipus rejects the help and advice of others who would help him, including Creon, Teiresias, and Jocasta. Janie's grandmother in *Their Eyes Were Watching God* is her first friend and guide even though Janie rejects her advice. Several others offer Janie advice during her journey, but most of them are false friends. Phoenix is guided along the way by several strangers, including the man in the woods and the nurses at the medical facility in town. Nick, the narrator in *The Great Gatsby*, tries to help Gatsby and gives him advice. In the end, Gatsby ignores this advice and is alone.

8. *The hero descends into darkness.*

The darkness is often both a physical and a spiritual state. In the Sumerian epic, Gilgamesh travels into the dark woods looking for Humbaba, guardian of the forest. He has another descent into darkness when he dives into the dark waters to get the plant of eternal life. Oedipus is figuratively in the dark when he is searching for the cause of the city's distress. In the end, he is literally in the dark when he blinds himself. Janie journeys to the "muck," the dark land around Lake Okechobee. Here she descends into physical darkness during the hurricane and loses her husband because of the storm, resulting in an emotional darkness. In Welty's short story, "A Worn Path," Phoenix must travel through the darkness of the woods and falls down into a ditch on her trek to town. Gatsby travels with his "friends" through the Valley of Ashes to go into town. The events that follow lead to his ultimate demise.

9. *The hero is not the same after emerging from the darkness of his or her descent.*

Gilgamesh is despondent at the loss of his friend and changes his quest after his first descent into darkness. After his final descent into darkness, Gilgamesh accepts that man is mortal. Oedipus cannot face his life after his descent into figurative and literal darkness, and therefore becomes an exile. Janie loses her final companion, Teacake, in the darkness of the hurricane and learns that she does not need another person to define herself. Phoenix receives a material reward out of her fall on the darkness, some money to spend on a present for her grandson, and a spiritual reward in the form of help from others. She also learns something about herself—that she is capable of going against her own values in order to help someone she loves. On the way back to Long Island through the Valley of Ashes, the accident with Gatsby's car occurs. He then learns that Daisy is not the ideal person he imagined.

10. *What the hero seeks is usually no more than a symbol of what he or she really finds.*

After Enkindu dies at the hands of Humababa, Gilgamesh believes that his quest is now the search for eternal life. As his quest for eternal life fails, Gilgamesh learns the importance of being a true leader and living a moral life. Oedipus' search for the person who killed the king and caused unhappiness in the city is really a quest to find his true self. Janie no longer searches for a man in order to define herself and to be happy. Phoenix learns the depth of what she is capable of doing to help her grandson. Gatsby learns his ideal woman is not perfect.

11. *The hero suffers a wound.*

Wounds can be physical, emotional, or psychological. Sometimes they are all three. Gilgamesh's greatest wound is the loss of his close friend Enkidu. Oedipus' physical wound is the self-inflicted one that takes his eyesight. Janie suffers beatings at the hands of her husband, and Phoenix falls into a ditch and is stranded on her back until a stranger comes along. On the emotional level, Phoenix suffers the wounds of prejudice inflicted by comments made by white people to her. Jay Gatsby dies of a gunshot wound.

12. *Mythological heroes tend to be males.*

In classical Greek and Roman mythology, heroes are typically male. More modern literature, however, has redefined the concept of the hero. Today, a hero in literature can be male or female, and the journey can be less of a physical one and more of a spiritual or psychological one. In her book, *The Heroine's Journey*, Maureen Murdock claims: "Women do have a quest. . . . It is the quest to fully embrace their feminine nature, learning how to value themselves as women so as to heal the deep wound of the feminine (1990, 3). There can be multiple layers to a woman's quest. Gilgamesh and Oedipus represent the classical model of a hero, while Janie and Phoenix represent a modern female model of a hero. Gatsby represents a modern male hero.

In teaching the hero's quest, we have added to Stillman's list the following characteristic found in Campbell's original work:

13. *Frequently, the hero returns to the everyday world to share his or her knowledge with others or to bring to consciousness new and better ways of living.*

Gilgamesh returns as a more moral and understanding king than he was at the beginning of the epic. Upon his return, he shares his new vision with the people of Uruk. Oedipus brings knowledge to his people when he discovers that he is the cause of the blight on his city. In doing so, however, Oedipus must exile himself from his home. At the end of *Their Eyes Were Watching God*, Janie tells her friend Phoebe what she has learned about life: People have to make their own journeys and learn for themselves. No one can do it for them. "A Worn Path" ends with Phoenix proudly carrying an unexpected present home to her grandson. With the death of Gatsby, it is up to his friend, Nick, to spread the message of what he learned about people.

Works Cited

Allen, Graham. 2000. *Intertextuality: The New Critical Idiom*. New York: Routledge.

Anderson, Richard C. 1977. "The Notion of Schemata and the Educational Enterprise." In R. C. Anderson, R. J. Spiro, and W. E. Montague (Eds.). *Schooling and the Acquisition of Knowledge*, 415–32. Hillsdale, NY: Erlbaum.

Barthes, Roland. 1975. *The Pleasure of the Text*. London: Jonathan Cape.

Beach, R. W., D. Applebaum, and S. Dorsey, 1990. "Adolescents' Use of Intertextual Links to Understand Literature." In R. Beach and S. Hynds (Eds.), *Developing Discourse Practices in Adolescence and Adulthood*, 224–45, Norwood, NJ: Ablex.

Beach, Richard, D. Applebaum, and S. Dorsey, 1994. "Adolescents' Use of Intertextual Links to Understand Literature." In H. Singer and R. B. Ruddell (Eds.), *Theoretical Models and Processes of Reading*, 695–714. Newark, DE: International Reading Association.

Bloome, David. 2003. "President's Update: Reading Comprehension as Intertextual Practice." *The Council Chronicle*, November: 3: 2, 13. Urbana, IL: National Council of Teachers of English.

Bloome, David, and Ann Egan-Robertson. 1993. "The Social Construction of Intertextuality in Classroom Reading and Writing Lessons." *Reading Research Quarterly* 28 4: 304–33.

Bressler, Charles E. 1994. *Literary Criticism: An Introduction to Theory and Practice.* Englewood Cliffs, NJ: Prentice Hall.

Campbell, Joseph. 1971. *The Hero with a Thousand Faces.* Princeton, NJ: Princeton University Press.

Chandler, Daniel. "Semiotics for Beginners." See www.aber.ac.uk/media/Documents/S4B/sem09.html. Accessed November 19, 2003.

Dreiser, Theodore. 2000. *An American Tragedy.* New York: Penguin Putnam.

Eldridge, David. 2005. *Hamlet* and *Rosencrantz and Guildenstern Are Dead.* See http://hsc.csu.edu.au/english/advanced. Composition study accessed January 6, 2005.

Gere, Anne Ruggles. 2001. "Dorthea Lange to the 'Boss': Versions of *The Grapes of Wrath.*" In Anne Ruggles Gere and Peter Shaheen, Eds., *Making American Literatures in College and High School*, 170–77. Urbana, IL: National Council of Teachers of English.

Gonzalez, April. 2004. *An Intertextual Approach to Teaching Hamlet.* Unpublished manuscript.

Hartman, David K. 1995. "Eight Readers Reading: The Intertextual Links of Proficient Readers Reading Multiple Passages." *Reading Research Quarterly* 30: 520–61.

Hartman, David K. 2004. "Deconstructing the Reader, the Text, the Author, and the Context." In *Uses of Intertextuality in Classroom and Educational Research*, 353–71. Greenwich, CT: Information Age Publishing.

Hero's Quest. 2004. See http://trickster.org. Accessed January 1, 2004.

Jung, Carl. 1998. "The Concept of the Collective Unconscious." In Robert A. Segal (Ed.), *Jung on Mythology*, 57–59. Princeton, NJ: Princeton University Press.

King, Stephen. 2002. "Why We Crave Horror Movies." In *The Prose Reader*, 452–57. Upper Saddle River, NJ: Pearson Education.

Kristeva, Julie. 1980. *Desire in Language: A Semiotic Approach to Literature and Art* (T. Gora, A. Jardin, and L. S. Rudiz, trans.). New York: Columbia University Press.

Lenski, Susan Davis. 1998. "Intertextual Intentions: Making Connections Across Texts." *Clearinghouse* 72 2: 74–80.

McBride, James. 2002. *The Color of Water*. New York: Penguin Putnam.

Many, Joyce E. 1996. "Patterns of Selectivity in Drawing on Sources: Examining Students' Use of Intertextuality Across Literacy Events." *Reading Research and Instruction* 36: 51–63.

Many, Joyce E., and D. L. Anderson. 1992. "The Effects of Grade and Stance on Readers' Intertextual and Autobiographical Responses to Literature." *Reading Research and Instruction* 31: 60–69.

Mellor, Bronwyn, Annette Patterson, and Marnie O'Neill. 2000. *Reading Fictions: Applying Literary Theory to Short Stories*. Urbana, IL: National Council of Teachers of English.

Murdock, Maureen. 1990. *The Heroine's Journey: Woman's Quest for Wholeness*. Boston: Shambhala.

Probst, Robert. 2004. *Response & Analysis: Teaching Literature*. Portsmouth, NH: Heinemann.

Rosenblatt, Louise. 1976. *Literature as Exploration*. New York: Noble and Noble. (First published in 1938.)

Rosenblatt, Louise. 1978. *The Reader, the Text, the Poem*. Carbondale: Southern Illinois University Press.

Schultz, Harry. 2003. *Blanche's Chair in the Moon*, Unpublished manuscript.

Shaheen, Peter. 2001. "New Lives for Old Texts: Literary Pairings." In *Making American Literatures in College and High School*, 133–36. Urbana, IL: National Council of Teachers of English.

Short, Kathy. 2004. "Researching Intertextuality with Collaborative Classroom Environments." In *Uses of Intertextuality in Classroom and Educational Research,* 376. Greenwich, CT: Information Age Press.

Shuart-Faris, Nora, and David Bloome. 2004. *Uses of Intertextuality in Classroom and Educational Research.* Greenwich, CT: Information Age Press.

Smith, Frank. 1988. *Understanding Reading, Fourth Ed.* Hillsdale, NJ: Erlbaum.

Soto, Gary. 2002. "The Pie." In *Short Takes,* Elizabeth Penfield, Ed. 167–69. New York: Longman.

Steinbeck, John. 1992. "Introduction" by Robert DeMott. *The Grapes of Wrath,* vii–xliv. New York: Penguin Group.

Stillman, Peter, Ed. 1985. *Introduction to Myth.* Portsmouth, NH: Boynton/Cook.

Strickland, Kathleen. 1995. *Literacy, Not Labels.* Portsmouth, NH: Boynton/Cook.

Tannen, Deborah. 1999. "Lecturing and Listening." In Judith Naddell, John Langan, and Linda McMeniman (Eds.), *The Macmillan Reader,* 417–24. Needham Heights, MA: Allyn and Bacon.

Vygotsky, Lev. 1978. In M. Cole, V. John-Steiner, S. Scribner, and E. Souberman (Eds.), *Mind in Society.* Cambridge, MA: Harvard University Press.

Wiggins, Grant, and Jamie McTighe. 1998. *Understanding by Design.* Alexandria, VA: ASCD.

Wright, Richard. 1998. *Native Son.* (Introduction by Arnold Rampersad). New York: Harper Collins.

Index

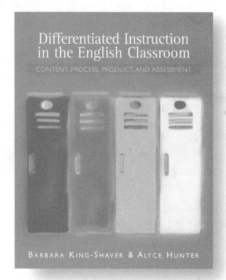